All Together!

Teaching music in groups

Project Consultants
Richard Crozier and Nigel Scaife

Project Editor
Anthony Marks

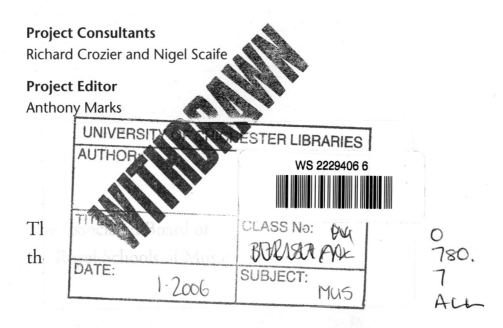

Th...

th...

First published in 2004 by
The Associated Board of the Royal Schools of Music (Publishing) Limited
24 Portland Place, London W1B 1LU, United Kingdom

© 2004 by The Associated Board of the Royal Schools of Music

ISBN 1 86096 398 6

AB 2939

A CIP catalogue for this book is available from The British Library.

Acknowledgements

Music and ICT Pack (p. 77)
Music Technology in Action (p. 78)
© Becta 1998
Reprinted by permission.

A small amount of other material used in Chapter 7 was first made available by Becta and is used here by permission.

A Common Approach 2002 (pp. 9, 122)
© 2002 by the Federation of Music Services and the National Association of Music Educators and the Royal College of Music
Reprinted by permission.

Susan Hallam: *Instrumental Teaching* (pp. 9, 21)
Reprinted by permission of Harcourt Education.

National Curriculum 2000 (pp. 69–70)
Crown Copyright material is reproduced with the permission of the Controller of HMSO and the Queen's Printer for Scotland.

Design and cover by Vermillion Design
Illustrations by John-Paul Early
Typeset by Hope Services (Abingdon) Ltd
Printed in England by Caligraving Ltd, Thetford, Norfolk

Foreword

Evelyn Glennie

Teachers have the power to shape lives and, in turn, to shape the world in which we live. The art of teaching is knowing how to improve things – how to bring about a better situation than existed earlier. This may sound simple, but it requires a formidable array of skills from teachers because they are always trying to reinvent, improve and inspire.

The publication of *All Together!* is without doubt a major statement of how we can reinvent, improve and inspire through the art of group music teaching. The inspiring contributors to the book draw upon their vast and diverse experience of group teaching, leaving no doubt that this is a vital route to awakening the joy in pupils' creative expression and knowledge. They show that group teaching allows teachers and pupils to take responsibility for their collective growth and open the doors of discovery for each other. In a group situation, teachers and pupils all tug, push and lead one another on to higher levels – and undoubtedly along the way this develops friendships, better understanding, patience and communication. These are priceless ingredients of all our lives.

I experienced group music teaching myself as a young girl. I was immersed in an environment of demonstration and inspiration from teachers and fellow pupils which enabled me to develop as a human being and led to my being better able to teach myself. I am delighted that the vital information in this important publication – the first of its kind – will reach so many of our schools and Music Services. In this age of universal communication I know it will quickly be shared worldwide. Let's keep remembering: we all assist each other in the art of discovery.

Contents

About the contributors

Chapter authors

Richard Crozier worked as a school music teacher, music co-ordinator and inspector in Avon and Bedfordshire before joining the ABRSM in 1995. He was course director for the ABRSM's Certificate of Teaching professional development course, and is now director of professional development. His publications include *Offbeat* (Heinemann, 1987) and (with Paul Harris) *The Music Teacher's Companion* (ABRSM Publishing, 2000).

Jo Glover has taught music in school, youth music, community and higher education settings. She is currently senior research fellow in music education at the University of Central England, Birmingham. Her publications include *Children Composing 4–14* (Routledge Falmer, 2000).

Carole Jenner-Timms studied at the Royal College of Music and is an accomplished flautist, teacher and woodwind tutor. She is the head of Bath and North East Somerset Music Service, and has been a mentor for the ABRSM's Certificate of Teaching professional development course since its inception in 1995.

Brian Ley was head of Gloucestershire Music Service from 1997 to 2002. He was a member of the advisory group to revise the National Curriculum for Music (1995) and of the working party that published *A Common Approach*. He was chair of the Music Advisers' National Association (1995–6) and vice-chair of the Music Education Council (1998–2003). He now works as an independent music-education consultant.

Lucinda Mackworth-Young is a consultant in psychology, pianist and teacher. She lectures and writes for professional development courses run by the ABRSM, the Incorporated Society of Musicians, the European Piano Teachers Association, education authorities, music colleges and universities. Through her association Music, Mind and Movement, she runs courses and in 2001 published her highly successful book *Tuning In*.

Nigel Scaife graduated from the Royal College of Music with a Masters degree in performance studies. He received a D.Phil from Oxford University in 1997 and thereafter worked as a teacher, performer and writer on music. As Syllabus Principal at the ABRSM he has led a number of major initiatives, including the introduction of the jazz horns syllabus and Music Medals.

Leo Turner works for the Solihull Music Service as a guitar teacher, ensemble director, curriculum support teacher and teaching coach. He frequently gives in-service training for several Music Services, and is a mentor for the ABRSM's Certificate of Teaching professional development course and an examiner for the London College of Music.

Teacher-contributors

Kathy Blackwell (KB – strings) works as a violin and viola teacher for Oxfordshire County Music Service. She was a strings consultant for the ABRSM's Music Medals. She is co-author of the *Fiddle Time* and *Cello Time* series, published by OUP.

Paul Cameron (PC – percussion) studied at the Royal College of Music before joining the Royal National Theatre as percussionist and musical director. His teaching roles include a professorship at the Royal Military School of Music. He is a mentor for the ABRSM's Certificate of Teaching professional development course. His series *Beat It!*, written with Evelyn Glennie, is published by Faber Music.

Toussaint Clarke (TC – steel pans) has been playing and making pans for almost forty years. He teaches and arranges for several bands in south-west England, and makes and tunes pans for musicians throughout Europe. He currently plays with the Rainbow Steel Orchestra in Bath.

Rebecca Crosby (RC – guitar) studied guitar at the Royal Northern College of Music, and is the lead teacher of guitar for Kirklees Music School. She has a special interest in teaching young beginners and coaching ensembles. She was a contributor to the classical guitar section of *A Common Approach 2002*.

Andrew Eales (AE – keyboards) works for Milton Keynes Music Service, where he leads the keyboard faculty and teaches in several schools. He is author of *Keyquest*, a series of four keyboard tutor books, and the keyboard ensemble music book *Keyband!*

Heidi Pegler (HP – singing) is head of singing at St Paul's Girls' School, London. She is an examiner for the ABRSM, and was a voice consultant for *A Common Approach 2002*. She is publicity officer for the Association of Teachers of Singing.

Richard Pepper (RPe – woodwind) was head of woodwind for the county of Avon for thirteen years. He then spent ten years as Director of the Royal Oman Symphony Orchestra. He is now head of the Cambridge area for the Cambridgeshire Instrumental Music Agency.

Robert Priestley (RPr – brass) worked for over twenty years in Berkshire, progressing from general brass teacher to regional head, teaching mostly in groups and directing ensembles. He now works in Coventry as a deputy head of the Performing Arts Service.

Mark Ray (MR – piano) is a pianist, teacher, examiner and writer. He is head of the School of Keyboard Studies at the Royal Northern College of Music and vice-chair of the European Piano Teachers Association (UK). He has given masterclasses in the UK, Singapore, Ukraine and Australasia.

Richard Wright (RW – guitar) is a freelance guitarist and teacher. He was the classical guitar co-ordinator for *A Common Approach 2002* and a consultant for the ABRSM's Music Medals. He gives in-service training to guitar teachers and is the editor of *The EGTA Series*, the graded repertoire books published by Chanterelle Verlag.

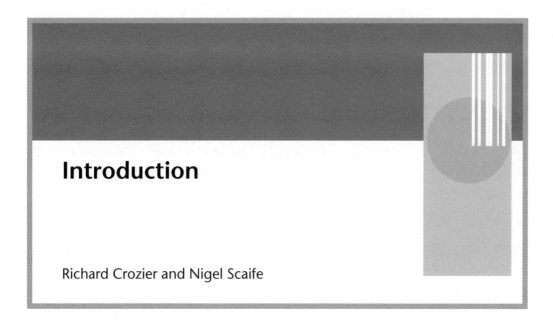

Introduction

Richard Crozier and Nigel Scaife

At the end of the nineteenth century, an important experiment in group teaching began at All Saints' School in Maidstone, Kent. A London-based music publisher and instrument manufacturer, J. G. Murdoch & Co., started a scheme which gave violin lessons to entire classes of schoolchildren. The company provided everything that was needed – violins and equipment, music and teaching materials, teachers and administration – and instruments and lessons were offered at low prices, payable in small instalments. After initial success in Maidstone, the company founded the Maidstone School Orchestra Association to aid promotion of the scheme, and later offered the same facilities for other instruments. At the height of its success, the organization provided lessons and instruments to almost 500,000 pupils in many parts of the UK (there were as many as 300 violin classes in London alone). This activity ceased with the outbreak of World War I, though not before it had inspired a number of visiting American educators to establish similar schemes in the USA.

Group and ensemble teaching continued to flourish during the twentieth century, though it was often viewed with scepticism. In 1927 John Borland, the music inspector for London County Council, reported that when violin classes were started in schools:

> Some said it was impossible to teach the violin in class; others said the classes would ruin the local violin teachers. These two criticisms seemed to 'cancel out'. A few years' experience showed that it was possible to teach the violin in class, and also that class-work stimulated scores of children to take solo lessons who would never have thought of learning the violin at all.
>
> (Borland, *Musical Foundations*, p. 64)

At the start of the twenty-first century, more teachers are turning to group work as more educational establishments require that children be taught in groups. While the progress towards the widespread adoption of group teaching in the United Kingdom may have been driven initially by financial and administrative imperatives as much as by educational ones – more children needing to be taught by fewer teachers in less time – it has long been clear that learning an instrument in a group has a great deal to offer pupils. Children enjoy making music with their friends and learning from each other. Group teaching aids the early development of ensemble and associated listening skills, and provides opportunities for creative work (often linked with classroom music activities). Clearly these advantages have a place alongside the long-established benefits of one-to-one tuition.

This book is for anyone interested in the theory and practice of group teaching: for those with well-established group practices, for those who are relatively new to the discipline, and for those who are contemplating group work and are perhaps in need of a little reassurance. It will prove equally useful for teachers of instrumentalists or singers. It looks in detail at the special dynamics of group work, placing it in a wider educational context. It considers the ways in which group lessons are different from one-to-one: the mechanics of dealing with several pupils at once, of working with pupils of different ages and abilities, of giving attention to all the group members. But it also looks at the similarities between the two disciplines: how many of the skills already second nature to one-to-one teachers – encouraging practice, planning lessons, monitoring and assessing progress, and so on – can be modified for the group context. It is full of hints and tips, as well as many considered reflections about the processes, advantages and pitfalls of group teaching and learning. It is not essential to read the chapters in order – dipping in and out will prove equally effective.

The authors of the volume are music educators with extensive experience of group teaching (and of teaching group teachers). The authors' contributions are illustrated by the views of a number of teachers working across a wide range of vocal and instrumental disciplines. The teachers were asked to provide their own insight, experiences and anecdotes about group work by responding to questions about:

- Teaching and learning in groups
- Developing instrumental skills
- Developing musical skills
- Developing ensemble skills
- Encouraging and monitoring progress
- The challenges and rewards of group teaching

Their invaluable feedback has been incorporated in the book (in 'speech bubbles'). This has ensured that the day-to-day realities of group teaching situations are always to the fore, and that new ideas and approaches emerge. Taking this 'symposium' approach has also meant that views sometimes conflict – although there is more often agreement than disagreement.

All Together! is suitable for reading cover to cover or for browsing individual chapters or topics. Cross-references in the margin direct the user to other parts of the book – sometimes to entire chapters, sometimes to smaller, more specific sections – where a particular idea is further explained or expanded.

Children learning to make music in groups have to develop a particular range of skills: listening sensitively to others; absorbing and processing musical information and reacting to it; staying together in ensembles; 'following on', developing or changing the ideas of their colleagues; and collaborating and negotiating to produce effective musical outcomes. Of course, each of these has a significant musical value in its own right and will set pupils up for lifelong enjoyable music-making. But in gaining these skills, group-taught pupils are also acquiring the fundamentals of interpersonal communication: they are learning to become part of a community. Through learning an instrument in a group, pupils are in fact learning citizenship – how to live in society. This is education in its most fundamental form.

The dynamics of group teaching

Brian Ley

In the past few decades music education has advanced on many fronts. The curriculum has evolved for both classroom and instrumental music, each building upon previous best practice. Changing perceptions of the nature and role of music have also influenced curriculum development. As a result, children and even adults – through lifelong learning opportunities – can now receive a music education that encompasses a wide range and variety of musical experiences, from general classroom music to specialist instrumental tuition and ensemble coaching.

Classroom music activities engage all pupils between the ages of 5 and 14 (and many beyond this age) in areas of musical experience that require them to listen and to apply their knowledge and understanding through practical activities. These activities promote the development of musical skills – controlling sounds through singing and playing, creating and developing ideas, and responding to and reviewing work. Alongside this, the instrumental programme caters for a smaller but not insignificant number of those who display aptitude, ability or interest in learning to play a musical instrument. Such a programme is generally delivered either by visiting specialist teachers in schools or by private teachers working independently from their own homes or studios. The music curriculum and the instrumental programme are often supplemented by extra- and extended-curricular ensemble activities. These take place outside the framework of the school timetable, sometimes in schools or in local music centres. Such activities provide additional opportunities for pupils and adults at different stages of musical development. They allow learners to come together to refine and develop their skills in ways which complement and extend the musical experiences they receive in class and in their instrumental lessons.

These three aspects – classroom experience, instrumental tuition and ensemble playing – are interrelated strands of a whole music-education programme, the benefits of one being enhanced and supported by the others. The extension from the classroom experience to instrumental tuition is being offered to more and more pupils as the demand grows. This growth has arisen partly because so many more parents want their children to learn to play a musical instrument. But it is also because there is recognition, from government and from music educators and researchers, of the value that learning to play a musical instrument brings, both intrinsically – through the development of musical skills, knowledge and understanding – and extrinsically – through the contribution that learning music makes to other key skills.

Increased demand has led to increased provision, though not necessarily merely 'more of the same'. The tradition of offering tuition on Western classical instruments has expanded over the past few years to include contemporary guitar, drums, keyboards, steel pans, African drums and Asian instruments. This has led to a consideration of the different teaching styles that are used in these new disciplines. It has also challenged assumptions about whether learning is best developed through individual tuition or in groups.

Group tuition in context

So many human activities take place within groups. Many of us inhabit workplaces alongside others with whom we share a common commitment. We interact in and through family groups. Beyond this, we often engage in recreational activities with others in team games, clubs or musical ensembles. In the same way, most educational activities that take place either within or outside the normal school timetable place pupils in situations where they work together, sharing common learning goals and often being required to work as a whole class or in smaller groups.

In the broader educational context the frequent and sustained one-to-one encounter between a teacher and learner is less common. In the area of instrumental training, however, it remains widespread, among those who are receiving tuition from private teachers and those, deemed particularly gifted, who receive their tuition in schools, places of higher education and music conservatoires. Often, though not always, this model of one-to-one teaching has a historical basis, formulated on what is described by Harris and Crozier (*The Music Teacher's Companion*) as the 'master–apprentice' principle. Group tuition, as an alternative model of instrumental and vocal instruction, often occurs in schools or in locally administered music centres and is regarded by some as being second best.

Yet learning in groups is not a new phenomenon. In the United States whole-group teaching in wind bands and orchestras has been long established, as has group piano instruction. In the United Kingdom, too, group teaching has been an integral part of musical tuition for a considerable time.

The emergence of instrumental group teaching in schools happened perhaps rather more by accident than design. In the United Kingdom, local authorities found themselves with generous amounts of Government money (with which they could buy instruments) and a lot of enthusiastic pupils – but not enough teachers.... Thus, teaching in groups offered itself as a solution by default to a difficult problem.

(Harris and Crozier, *The Music Teacher's Companion*, p. 80)

In the half-century since the setting-up of Local Education Authority (LEA) Music Services, which brought in this group teaching approach, the argument of administrative expediency has been somewhat replaced by that of financial expediency. Now parents are generally required to pay for their children's instrumental tuition, whether it is delivered privately or in school. Pro rata, group tuition is less expensive than individual tuition and may therefore be more attractive to the paying client. But alongside administrative and financial considerations lies another, arguably more powerful, educational reason for the continued growth and development of group instrumental tuition. The increasing benefits of group teaching are now recognized and demonstrated through the imaginative approaches of a growing number of committed teachers. These people appreciate the value of individual tuition at certain stages of a pupil's development but they also understand the huge potential of the interaction that takes place between pupil and pupil as well as that between pupil and teacher. Group tuition provides stimulating challenges and exciting rewards. It is not a second-best approach, nor is it a compromise in order to accommodate a growing number of learners.

This chapter and the six that follow it illustrate some of the most effective characteristics of group tuition in action. A number of highly respected teachers (of strings, woodwind, brass, electronic keyboard, piano, guitar, percussion, steel pans and the voice) have shared and documented their experiences of group teaching and learning. They have highlighted the benefits and rewards of this approach as well as its challenges and pitfalls. They have outlined the methods and styles they adopt in group work. Together they provide invaluable insight into this approach to instrumental and vocal teaching. Their observations will stimulate and encourage good practice, both for those already teaching in groups and for those considering introducing group tuition into their timetable.

The group dynamic

Any educational encounter is enhanced and fulfilled when the relationship between the teacher and learner promotes, supports and encourages musical learning. The rapport that is established in one-to-one teaching may differ from that in group teaching, but in both instances it is essential to set up a conducive learning environment that will facilitate the most effective responses and promote musical understanding. So in what ways does teaching an instrument in a group differ from teaching it one-to-one? A reason cited by a number of the teachers is that of the 'dynamic' of group teaching.

> Group teaching has a different 'dynamic' from individual lessons. In my experience, different-sized groups have a completely different feel: groups of two can be hard work, whereas groups of four can be much easier as the group dynamic takes over. Medium-sized groups (7–12) are different again as they share the characteristics of both group and class situations. After that, when you get to half a class and larger (say 15 or more), you are giving a class lesson and the techniques tend to be different again.
>
> The one-to-one situation is very unusual for children in modern education. They are used to working as a class or as a small group within the class. The one-to-one situation has the potential to be too intense, and to generate too much pressure and pace. Children tend to benefit from the positive atmosphere generated in the group situation; they feel safe with their peers, and do not feel so intimidated and isolated as they know they are sharing the experience. It is all too easy for the individual lesson to abandon music and concentrate on technique and negative correction ('No, not like that!'). In groups, however, one can use members of the group as role models ('See how James has his thumb in the right place'). This has the benefit both of praising the role model and of helping the others to see that one of their peers can do it right.
>
> The teacher can use pupils as examples of good (and bad) practice – visually and aurally. The group dynamic can encourage the pupils to progress. Group or peer support is a powerful medium, and I find that in the group situation it is much easier to have fun while still pushing the lesson forward. Understanding can be fostered when group members listen to others explaining points (rather than the teacher); group pupils also benefit from seeing technical issues worked through by peers with the same-sized hands and with similar co-ordination and strength problems. There are times when the teacher's technical competence can make it difficult to demonstrate adequately; watching and listening to peers can be very helpful in this situation. Mutual support and praise from peers are very effective.   RPr

Critical to the success of this type of teaching and learning is the way in which the group dynamic is established, developed and supported. In a group lesson, pupils can learn from each other, often as much as or more than they do from the teacher. The role of the teacher is therefore different from that in an individual lesson. The master–apprentice teaching style is replaced by one that encourages peer support and develops independent learning. As always, developing good relationships with the pupils is essential. In a group situation, though, the balance of the relationship changes.

9

Psychology of group teaching

In an individual lesson, the relationship between teacher and pupil is particularly important to the success of the teaching and learning. Where the relationship is good, a positive outcome is more likely, although there is a danger that teacher and pupil can spend too large a proportion of the lesson time in general chit-chat rather than music-making. Where the relationship between teacher and pupil is less good, this will be particularly detrimental, and could lead to the pupil giving up music altogether. 'Not liking the teacher' is a commonly cited reason for pupils giving up learning a musical instrument.

The balance of relationships within group tuition is clearly different, with the dominance of the teacher–pupil relationship less paramount. The key here is for the teacher to relate to the group as a whole in a more general sense. Relationships between the pupils themselves play as important a role in ensuring that they each enjoy their time learning music. This is arguably a far more healthy relationship model, fitting more naturally into the overall emotional life of most children.

Relationships within the group provide a stimulus which, if harnessed with care by the teacher, will lead to the maximized involvement and engagement of all the pupils, with interpersonal conflict and personality clashes between teacher and pupil kept to an absolute minimum. I would expect pupils learning within groups to be far less likely to cite 'not liking the teacher' as their reason should they later give up learning music.

AE

The group dynamic can, of course, affect the way in which the teacher responds and acts as much as it affects the pupils. Good teachers will recognize the positive impact that group discussion and peer learning can have, and they will adapt their teaching style to encompass the roles of facilitator and enabler, allowing, where appropriate, pupils to take control and to develop independence in their learning.

Group tuition encourages a group feeling and responsibility. The focus of comment is diffused, so all members of the group can evaluate performance results and objectives. How it sounded as opposed to how it felt can be discussed. The teacher can replace one pupil in the group and ask him or her to act as critic. The music still remains intact.

Fundamentally, there is no difference in terms of objectives between teaching small groups and teaching individuals. However, the group situation does allow for more variety and flexibility within a lesson.

RPe

Facing the challenges, reaping the rewards

Teaching pupils, students and adults in groups is not an exclusive activity, and there are stages when individual tuition is an equally beneficial method of instruction; indeed there are occasions when the two activities are mutually interactive.

> In some ways teaching in groups is similar to class teaching – instruction is geared towards a whole group or class rather than to one individual. Having said that, good group teaching should be a mixture of individual and group teaching; the differing needs of each one in the group need to be met within the context of the group situation. This, alongside the limited time available (usually half an hour), is the most challenging aspect of group teaching.   KB

The purpose of this book (and especially the following chapters, where group tuition is outlined in action) is not to advocate group tuition exclusively, nor to highlight the disadvantages of individual tuition: they are mutually supportive activities. It is, rather, to outline the best practice in group tuition in order to encourage its use as another, perhaps prime, means of raising musical standards and supporting musical improvement.

There are significant advantages of teaching in groups and there are challenges and rewards for both teachers and learners. Susan Hallam identifies a number of advantages of the group-teaching approach. Group teaching can:

- be more stimulating for teachers and pupils;
- provide more opportunities for demonstrating alternative methods and strategies;
- provide more opportunities for critical evaluation, both musical and technical;
- foster independent learning in pupils;
- be more fun;
- provide opportunities for informal performance to assist with overcoming nervousness;
- help shy children to feel less inhibited playing with others.

(Hallam, *Instrumental Teaching*, p. 253)

Comments from pupils themselves endorse some of these views:

I enjoy group lessons. I can learn from the mistakes of others. Also, I find it helpful to have my playing criticized constructively by my friends. It's fun playing quartets in lessons.

(*A Common Approach 2002*, p. 15)

Other comments from pupils indicated the benefit of advice given and received by others – and not just the teachers – and the setting of targets and the comparison of performance with others in the group.

Among the challenges to successful group work are those related to planning, the development of technique, catering for individual needs within a group, and effective monitoring and assessment. The following chapters attempt to address these and many other issues, not least the musical and educational rewards of group teaching. But alongside the musical learning that takes place in group lessons there are often other significant rewards.

Early in my group-teaching career I learnt that group tuition has some educational and musical advantages over individual lessons; but it can have secondary benefits that could be considered even more important. The following story shows an example of this:

When I first began teaching in one particular school I was told by the music co-ordinator that one of the pupils being sent my way had special needs. It transpired that these needs related to behaviour and social interaction. The boy in question – who I shall call David – was unable to relate to his peers, and his normal behaviour in class was to be isolative and avoid all other human contact. When he felt his personal space was threatened he would respond violently, and had already been permanently excluded from a previous school. He had expressed an interest in learning the keyboard but the school was a little concerned that working within a small group could be problematic for him. It hoped, however, that keyboard lessons could in fact help him to turn a corner socially and begin to interact positively with others.

Within a few weeks it became clear that this more positive prognosis would prove true. David began to integrate with the other members of the group. Although initially reserved, he soon joined in the group games and activities with enthusiasm, and took great pride in the small progress he made as a keyboard player. According to his class teacher he also began to talk in class about how much he was enjoying his keyboard lessons, breaking his normal silence to do so. After a year of lessons David had made little progress as a keyboard player, and decided not to continue learning. However, his personality had been radically altered for the better, and according to feedback from the school it was his group keyboard lessons that provided the main initial catalyst for this transformation.   AE

In conclusion

Our knowledge of the nature and role of music education has developed with our understanding of the value that music has to us as human beings. Instrumental tuition plays a significant part in enhancing and developing the knowledge, skills and understanding that are experienced in the general music class. Such tuition can be provided on a one-to-one basis, and this may be appropriate at some stages of learning; however, group tuition is now recognized as an essential part of a complete learning experience.

One of the characteristics of good teaching is the creation of an atmosphere that enables the most effective learning to take place. In such an atmosphere, a dynamic is established that drives the whole process of teaching and learning how to play a musical instrument.

Music is a social skill. It is about sharing enjoyment and performance. It is communication, sensitivity to others, reaction to others, helping others, being helped by others. Singing together and dancing together are popular pursuits. Playing an instrument is part of this. I pity the pupil who learns on their own, who plays to the bedroom wall and sticks their examination certificates on it.

The skills of working together, literally in harmony, are skills for all aspects of life, and music is a wonderful medium for this. Very few of our pupils are going to be soloists but all will need the support of other musicians if they wish to enjoy their music-making. Group tuition includes this most important aspect from the beginning.

RPe

...the pupil who plays to the bedroom wall...

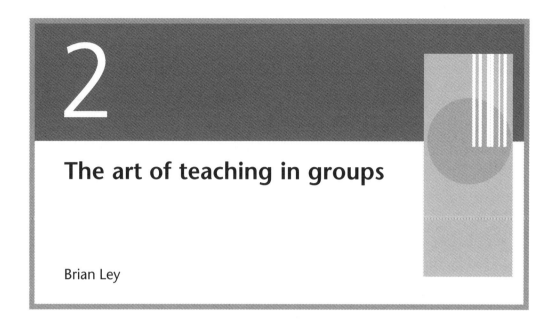

The art of teaching in groups

Brian Ley

The art of teaching has been described as being akin to conducting an orchestra, where all the separate strands of music are kept in synchrony (Kyriacou, *Effective Teaching in Schools*). This musical analogy seems as appropriate to instrumental teaching as it does to classroom teaching, and more especially to group work, where sensitivity to the overall progress of a lesson and to the contributions and needs of all members of the group is crucial to effective teaching.

Teaching and learning

As teachers, our prime aim is to enable learning to take place. But it is not a one-way process, in which the teacher imparts particular skills and information to pupils, who then assimilate and regurgitate them. Teaching and learning are mutually dependent. The task of the teacher is to set up exciting and varied activities so that learners are able to develop real understanding of what they know, of what they can do and of how they can improve their performance. Good instrumental teachers, whether working one-to-one or in groups, will engage and lead pupils in rich musical experiences that motivate them to continue to learn. Put simply, what happens in the half-hour of teacher–pupil contact in the lesson will stimulate musical activity and learning, through practice, during the rest of the week. So the way we teach needs to take account of and be influenced by the way our pupils learn.

Ways of learning

In recent years, specialized research has provided real insights into the relationship of the two hemispheres of the brain and of the importance of the interaction of brain functions. In *The Sounding Symbol* George Odam provides well-documented evidence in this field, outlining music education's uniqueness as schooling for the whole brain, involving the processes of both the left hemisphere (the objective and analytical) and the right hemisphere (the subjective and holistic). He proposes that, in instrumental tuition, teachers and children should be aware of which parts of their brains can do which kinds of task. He further suggests that the establishment of acute and analytical listening skills, together with a creative approach to interpretation, reinterpretation and invention, is as much a part of good music teaching and learning as the development of technique.

Understanding learning

p. 98 →

But the technique-driven approach still often dominates instrumental lessons. One reason for this has been the false perception on the part of so many teachers that the instrumental curriculum should be dictated by the requirements of graded examinations. The course of study undertaken by pupils has, more often than not, been influenced by the syllabuses from the various major examination boards. Here, requirements focus mainly on technical control of the instrument (or, in the case of singing, the voice), performance skills, sight-reading, aural skills and a knowledge of theory; requirements which, for most examination purposes, are unrelated to each other. For many teachers, the syllabus for a particular graded examination has determined what the pupil studies, taking little account of the nature of learning or of broader aspects of music education. It has often resulted in a fragmentary curriculum for those receiving such tuition, since the examination has influenced rather than reflected the practice of instrumental teaching. This is not to be critical of an examination process that is well established and provides achievable goals and motivation for so many learners. But summative assessment in the form of examinations, at whatever stage of learning, demonstrates what the candidate knows and can do; it should not dictate how the learner is taught. An over-reliance on 'teaching to the exam' denies pupils access to a broader and richer curriculum, one which can still provide a secure basis for the examination requirements but which will also cater for the growing number who learn in groups and for whom the individual graded examination may be less relevant.

But things are changing. Teachers recognize that group teaching requires different styles and strategies, and the introduction of new assessments such as Music Medals provides a fresh approach for instrumentalists who are taught in groups. In addition, and perhaps more importantly, as music teachers – both classroom practitioners and instrumental specialists – we now better understand the different ways in which learning takes place. We recognize that some of our pupils learn best from doing, others from listening and others from visual stimuli. Each pupil will have a different combination of these strengths. Most of us now accept that an exclusive 'I tell you and you do' approach is narrow and takes little account of the interactive nature of teaching and learning. Instrumental teachers now recognize the importance of understanding

16

Music Medals

the learning process and of adapting their teaching to take account of the variety of ways in which we learn.

> In the classroom, teachers have successfully developed a wide range of teaching strategies to maximize the learning potential of students across the whole spectrum of learning preferences.
>
> Our approach to instrumental teaching, like that of our classroom colleagues, must also be sufficiently varied and stimulating across the range of these preferences in order to be effective with as many of our pupils as possible. Our pupils are used to learning in a classroom environment where modern research into teaching and learning has been fully absorbed.
>
> Group lessons bring this imperative closer to reality and this is perhaps one of the most vital reasons that group tuition is proving so much more effective with our pupils in schools today than individual lessons previously have. AE

Instrumental teaching and learning in action

Group teaching is not a pale substitute for individual work. It requires the teacher to provide a different educational experience that engages each member of the group through listening, playing, sharing, discussing and evaluating. Good group teaching involves all pupils, all the time. To be effective, teaching will rely on good planning put into effective practice and influenced by proper monitoring and evaluation. This straightforward 'Plan, do, review' model can form the basis for organizing group tuition. Examples of the model in action are provided in this book by contributing teachers.

Planning

11

Lesson planning for groups

> It is probably true to say that (unless they are being inspected!) most instrumental teachers prepare for lessons mentally rather than writing formal lesson plans. However, this mental preparation is increasingly informed by the various planning templates which have been produced by Music Services, FMS, ABRSM and others in recent years. Such templates have helped instrumental teachers to reconsider the benefits of planning and particularly to think through the issues involved in preparing for group lessons. One particular result of this preparation has been that teachers have learnt to include a specific range of activities in lessons, rather than simply responding to the demands of an individual pupil. These activities will often

have a group focus. Ideally they will be holistic in nature, enabling more than one aspect of the instrumental curriculum to be incorporated within the activity. They will be fun for the group. A degree of differentiation is also likely to be built into the activities, enabling all to take part at an appropriate level.

Planning activities has been a major stimulus to instrumental teachers in recent years, enabling us both to re-evaluate and to reinvigorate our teaching practice.   AE

Planning for group tuition, then, is essential, not just in the week-by-week lesson but also in the medium-term plan for, say, a half-term's work; this is a critical aspect of planning. It is also important to have a long-term strategy, over a stage of musical development from one grade or level to another, or over a period of time like the school year: this may relate to, though not be dominated by, the graded examination syllabus. Published schemes of work such as *A Common Approach 2002* provide a framework for instrumental teaching and learning, and these have included templates for planning areas of musical experience and musical activities. Underpinning this is the opportunity for learners to experience music at first hand and to develop their musical understanding by:

- developing technique on their instrument or voice;
- listening;
- performing, both solo and with others;
- improvising, composing and communicating musical ideas;
- responding to and evaluating their own and others' work.

The emphasis of much instrumental tuition may focus on developing technique, and this is understandable, because the mastering of the technical control of an instrument or voice is a pre-requisite to the engagement in other musical activities. However, good teaching will encompass an integrated approach to musical learning in which each aspect of listening, performing, improvising, composing and appraising are fully integrated in a holistic way, or in what Harris and Crozier (*The Music Teacher's Companion*) describe as 'simultaneous learning'.

Doing

When planning is translated into practice, teachers have to consider the various methods and strategies that can have the most positive impact on learning. They also have to translate the long- and medium-term objectives in their plans into the short-term details of each weekly lesson. These details can be in note form, but should indicate particular learning aims and show how the various strands of the lesson are interlinked, so that learning in one part of the lesson is reinforced and leads seamlessly to another. So what are the characteristics of good, well-planned instrumental teaching, and how are these reflected in group practice?

Demonstrating and modelling

My lessons often start with my playing a short phrase to the class. All I tell them is the starting note. They copy this phrase back. If they have problems, I just repeat the phrase until they get the hang of it. I can then continue doing this as a group activity or play a phrase for each pupil to copy. I can tailor these to the level of each player, making sure they can all succeed. Pupils can take the lead and offer their own invented phrase to another member of the group.

This technique can be useful as an introduction to a new scale. The scale builds up in short manageable sections and employs a variety of fun rhythms. This can be continued the following week until the whole scale is learnt. The scale is learnt as an aural exercise combined with a tactile memory. The whole process is wordless, has a constant sense of pulse and can experiment with dynamic levels and a variety of articulation. The scale sheet is a memory jogger rather than a most uninviting challenge.

RPe

In this example, the teacher is encouraging the pupils to listen and copy as he plays a musical phrase. Within the activity, attention can also focus on posture, breathing and tone quality. But what is important to note here is that the teacher is demonstrating by actually playing his instrument to the group. It is essential that a teacher has technical mastery of an instrument, beyond the level at which it is taught, since effective teaching depends on demonstration. Good instrumental teachers, as musicians, provide models from which their students learn. That is not to say that, in group teaching where teachers may teach more than one type of instrument, they need to play at an advanced level in every discipline, but they should be good instrumentalists in their particular specialism. That is not to say, either, that demonstration and modelling by the teacher alone should dominate the lesson.

Modelling and appraising each other can be a useful learning tool. Ask someone in the group to demonstrate a particular technique – bow division in broken slurs, for example – and invite the others to comment on something specific such as 'How much bow did she use for the first note?' This can help students to analyse technical points and further develop their own understanding and playing.

KB

In addition to their own performing skills, teachers also need to have a secure command of the requirements of the course of study, including a knowledge of the technical demands of the instrument, the appropriate exercises and repertoire to reinforce such technical control, and the activities and games that will broaden and enhance musical learning through the development of listening, aural and creative skills.

In order for demonstration and modelling to work effectively, it is absolutely vital that pupils are encouraged to listen as well as look. Listening is fundamental to all musical experience.

From the very beginning, pupils should be encouraged to listen and react to the other musicians playing with them. Even if they are playing in unison they should be listening to the whole result, not just their own part. In a group lesson, these listening skills are still in place but the teacher can be freed from playing duties to focus more attention on the players. Any suggestions or solutions to problems can be demonstrated on one pupil while the others observe. Pupils can often see their problems more clearly in another player than in themselves, and can appreciate and use any solution quickly. Pupils can also admire the playing of their partners and try to emulate them.

RPe

Listening

p. 36 ➔

Using appropriate teaching strategies

Perhaps the most critical aspect of group teaching lies in the teacher's choice of methods and strategies to enable all pupils to learn effectively. These will vary according to the size and make-up of the group.

6

Encouraging progress

Pupils start singing lessons at many different levels and with different expectations. Some pupils are only interested in singing a particular kind of music, whether that be musical, pop, jazz or classical, while others are happy to have a go at all types. Some pupils are confident about performing in front of others; others are shy or inhibited. Some pupils can confidently sing in tune or have some musical awareness; others have difficulty with pitch making and find notated music alien or confusing. A group singing lesson can include students from many different areas, with different expectations, backgrounds and interests. Group teachers need to be organized and focused if they are to get the most out of the lesson time. They need to be flexible and aware of the needs of each individual pupil within the group.

HP

Children rarely make uniform progress, especially in learning to sing or play a musical instrument. This flexibility and awareness of individual needs, therefore, demands careful thought, and should direct which teaching strategies are employed so that every pupil is properly challenged.

Matching work to pupils' ability

p. 61 →

I find that the fastest learner in the group usually has a positive effect on the others, inspiring them to make quicker progress. It is less usual for the slower learner to have an adverse effect on the others. Sometimes, however, the slower learner will be discouraged, so it is important to provide differentiated material to enable all the pupils to learn at their own pace. Where differentiation becomes more marked, I would usually try to reorganize groups to provide a better match within each group in a school. The popularity of electronic keyboards makes this possible in most instances.

AE

Differentiation for musical ability may take several forms. Players could experiment with different pans to identify strengths and weaknesses. This could lead to increased one-to-one support if appropriate, or possibly smaller group work. It is also possible to use stronger players to support weaker players in small group situations. However, it is important to maintain awareness of weaker players so they don't become demoralized, and of stronger players so they don't become bored.

TC

…use stronger players to support weaker players…

Using questions

p. 120 →

There are many ways in which the group teacher can capture the interest and enthusiasm of all pupils: by providing clear explanations; by using a range of open and closed questions to stimulate discussion and extend learning among the whole group;

and by setting up musical activities in which all can take part and by which all can progress. Good group teaching encourages the participation of all members of the group while providing enough individual attention to those who need it. Achieving this balance is perhaps the greatest challenge for teachers, but group teaching is at its most effective when teachers find methods that motivate and inspire all pupils and where they employ strategies that reflect the different learning styles within the group. It does not mean working at the pace of the slowest.

The time in a group lesson has to be maximized so that the teacher can do a mixture of individual and group teaching. It is important to hear everyone do something on their own during each lesson, even if it is only one line or a few bars. However, when the teacher is working with an individual, the others in the group must be occupied. There are many different ways to do this:

One person in the group plays; the others follow the music and place their left-hand fingers without bowing. Or the rest of the group can play pizzicato while an individual bows. Or the rhythm, pulse or letter names are said, tapped or sung in turn as each person plays a small section of a piece. It is useful to change the activity as you move round the group so that interest is maintained.

Share the tune. Ask someone to start, and get the next person to take over at a given signal (this could be his or her name or the end of the phrase or line), and so on. This is especially useful for younger players. It keeps everyone listening and concentrating on following the music even if they are not actually playing.

Give a 'performance'. Ask someone to play on their own, giving the others something specific to comment on – dynamics or intonation, for example. Encourage constructive criticism: 'What was good and what could be improved upon?' Listeners could be asked to give marks out of 10 and say why. This encourages students to analyse the sounds that they hear. Listening in this active way to the others in their group helps develop their own playing.

Ask students to make up questions about the piece they are playing. In the group situation, these viva voce sessions are useful assessment times for the teacher, as well as reinforcing understanding for the students.

It can be helpful to use members of the group to demonstrate to each other – students are more focused if you ask someone to illustrate good posture or bow-hold.   KB

Supporting learning

The quality of our teaching will almost always affect what our pupils learn and the attitudes they bring to their learning. More often than not, good teaching results in good learning, where pupils respond well to the challenges and tasks set, show a willingness to work and make generally good progress in lessons and over time. In any instrumental lesson, our aim is to help pupils to acquire, develop and improve their musical skills and knowledge, and to increase their understanding by being active, independent learners. Active learning is most effective when pupils are fully engaged in the lesson and are able to work productively.

> Pupils learn to behave as musicians – participate, contribute and shape. Pupils can play a rhythm, then hear that rhythm picked up by other pupils and worked. They are then empowered to take that rhythm back and own it. Pupils can learn the function of different layers of rhythm – 'groove' and 'feel' rhythms, pulse rhythms, harmonic rhythms and melodic rhythms. In groups, learning can take place through listening rather than through reading. Of course this can be possible through good one-to-one teaching but it is often very teacher-directed.
>
> Group activities empower the pupils to participate and then contribute when feeling confident, to shape a future for the groove. Group members can change tempo, dynamic, time signature and feel. If they can change these structures, then they not only understand what they are but also the real-time function of how and when they work.   PC

Good group tuition encourages an active approach to learning. By its very nature, group teaching will involve pupils working together, collaboratively, and learning from each other as well as from the teacher. Interaction is a key to the success of group work. It supports the more holistic approach to teaching, where the development of technique forms only part of the process; it certainly does not prevent the teacher from providing individual help within the group. The model of the musical 'trainer' that has permeated so much instrumental tuition in the past is replaced by that of guide, coach, enabler and facilitator.

Active learning can help pupils to take control of what they do musically and to develop an autonomous and independent approach to their learning. As they become more experienced musicians, pupils will need to take more responsibility for their learning. They are then likely to be better motivated and, therefore, to improve their performance. Susan Hallam suggests that it is possible to help even young pupils to develop some degree of independence, and that teachers need to encourage learners:

- to be unafraid to learn and be prepared to tackle tasks on their own;
- to have enjoyed learning and found it rewarding in its own right, not just to obtain some external goal;
- to be aware of their own strengths and weaknesses as learners;
- to be aware of the strategies that they have available for carrying out any number of tasks;
- to be able to assess what is required in a task;
- not to give up when the going gets tough and to have ideas about what they might do in those circumstances;
- to be able to evaluate their work and be critical of it;
- to want to improve their work;
- to be aware of important subjective issues in evaluation;
- to question what they are doing and why.

(Hallam, *Instrumental Teaching*, p. 239)

Reviewing

As a natural course of events instrumental teachers should, and in most cases do, monitor their work and the work of their pupils, and evaluate the success of their teaching. Evaluation is part of the planning and review process, which for much of the time is subconscious and intuitive. For example, following a lesson that has gone very well or even one in which things have gone less well, the teacher will probably analyse and reflect on what occurred. The results of this analysis will inform the approach and content of the next lesson: perhaps a change in the format of the lesson to provide a greater stimulus for the pupil. An increasing number of teachers keep notes on the outcome of the lesson, often incorporated within the lesson plan, in which they make brief comments about the standards that the pupils reach, and identify areas of improvement that are required for particular pupils. This forms a useful review of lessons.

Beyond this weekly monitoring of teaching, however, is the longer-term approach to self-evaluation. At the end of an academic year, or at a certain stage in the pupils' development, many teachers will reflect carefully on their practice over the period, identifying the most and least successful aspects of their work. Which areas of group tuition enabled the pupils to learn effectively? Were there any particular strategies that worked better than others? How can the pupils be helped to make better progress and raise musical standards further? In answering this type of question the teacher is able to consider the whole process of teaching and learning; such consideration can, more importantly, inform future planning. Self-evaluation, then, offers a secure basis for reviewing the plans and activities for group teaching. The 'plan, do, review' model thus becomes a useful tool for self-evaluation because it is cyclical and ongoing.

11

Lesson planning for groups

12

Assessment for groups

Being motivated

Instrumental teaching is challenging, time-consuming and sometimes frustrating; it can also be one of the most rewarding and satisfying occupations. The seemingly endless round of pupils receiving their half-hour lesson can be a daunting prospect, especially if the teaching happens in several places, with a great deal of travelling in between. As teachers, we can appreciate the benefits and ease of engaging with well-motivated pupils. We sometimes neglect the need to understand what motivates *us*. We are probably motivated when we feel valued, when our working conditions are conducive and when we know that our pupils are responding to us positively; when, in fact, *they* are motivated. Motivation is therefore a two-way process. When pupils feel valued they will often develop more confidence and self-esteem, be more open to learning and become more ambitious in their work. Pupils will be motivated to learn an instrument if it is seen as a relevant and enjoyable experience.

Motivation is likely to increase when the pupils understand why they are doing what they do, and this reinforces the need for proper planning by the teachers and the sharing of targets and goals of that planning. The teacher's musical leadership and inspiration, together with a varied approach which recognizes and is sympathetic to pupils' different learning styles, are key factors to motivation.

Motivation

p. 108 ➤

In conclusion

Instrumental teaching and learning in groups require teachers to make a particular commitment to their pupils, who may come to lessons with different approaches and bring different attitudes to their learning. The teacher's task is to promote and harness pupils' natural enthusiasm and to engage them in ways which motivate the whole group but which support the learning and progress of the individual.

The art of group teaching relies on some basic principles which underpin its successful organization and practice. Group teaching is at its most effective when:

- it fosters pupils' understanding and enjoyment of music through active involvement in practical activities that allow them to listen, to perform (sing and play), to be creative (improvise and compose) and to appraise their own and others' work;
- there is a secure framework for teaching and learning which provides a coherent and progressive course of study through the stages of musical development;
- the diversity of pupils' musical abilities within the group is catered for and each individual is appropriately supported.

Above all, instrumental tuition in general, and group tuition in particular, is at its best when music itself and the development of musical understanding are at the heart of the learning process.

3

Developing technical skills

Brian Ley

In the previous chapter, it was proposed that good instrumental teaching should focus on music itself and that our role, as teachers, is to foster and support pupils' musical understanding through activities that develop their musical skills and knowledge. In practice this means that instrumental teachers provide opportunities for their pupils to discover music at first hand by listening and through musical experiences that enable them to:

- perform (both solo and in ensemble);
- improvise and communicate their own musical ideas;
- compose;
- respond to and evaluate their own work and that of others.

Underpinning these musical experiences will be the development of technical control, for without this pupils will struggle to master their instrument. Technique will usually form the focal point of instrumental teaching, whether in one-to-one or in group work. But technique should serve the cause of music-making, not dictate it. The mastery of technique will remain sterile if it is taught in isolation from real musical experience and if pupils do not appreciate the mutually supportive relationship between the two. The balance may, of course, vary according to the age and ability of the learner: for example, in the early stages of playing the emphasis may be placed more on the actual music, with technical progress arising from the pieces studied. For more advanced pupils, there may be greater emphasis on technical work first, which is then reinforced through the pieces. But whatever the approach, the key to developing technique is in its relationship with actual musical experience.

This chapter draws upon the information provided by a number of expert and highly regarded instrumental teachers and leaders, who share the experiences of their own practice in developing technique within group work. In all cases, these teachers adopt a holistic approach so that technique relates to and develops from other musical experiences.

> At any stage, it is useful for pupils to understand the 'why' behind any technical activity, and where possible to relate it to another performing activity (repertoire, improvisation, composition).
>
> MR

Technique defined

There is a general consensus among the teacher-contributors about the key elements of technique, whatever the instrument in question. They are:

Preparation

Warm-ups, both vocal and instrumental, often form the preparation for the lesson. These can also help to establish a routine that pupils can use in their practice at home.

Posture

Attention to posture is an important pre-requisite to producing a good sound.

Producing a good sound

To enable good sound production, pupils need a range of skills, depending on the instrument in question: effective breathing, embouchure, bow-hold, hand position, fingering, and so on.

Intonation

Pupils should learn to listen, identify good and bad intonation, and adjust it where necessary to play in tune.

Articulation

The sound should be controlled and manipulated by means of appropriate co-ordination of hands, fingers and – depending on instrument – breath, bow, and so on.

These aspects of technique are not always tackled at the same time or in the same lesson, but they are systematically developed over time. In all cases the pupils are encouraged to play with feeling and expression so that the technical exercises are regarded as 'real music'.

Nurturing and developing technique

In practice, the development of technique does not differ between group and one-to-one teaching:

Technical skills are acquired in the same way whether in a group or individual lesson. Correct posture, finger positioning, articulation, breathing technique, special fingering, embouchure, and so on are taught and reinforced by the teacher. However, having a group of players can make the practice of these skills more fun.

RPe

There are, though, particular challenges in developing technique in a group context:

One has to be aware of technical issues at an individual level without letting them dominate the lesson for everyone. This involves a certain amount of physical movement by the teacher as well as more 'plate spinning' than in an individual lesson, as one keeps the group activity going while also concentrating on an individual problem. Obviously, general points of technique can be introduced as well and worked on with the whole group. This is an efficient use of time and the teacher can use peer observation to help ensure that the correct technique is being used. Peer comment can also help reinforce the points. It can be helpful to get the pupils to remind each other automatically about things like posture and hand position during the warm-ups at the beginning of lessons.

RPr

Preparation

Warm-up activities are an important feature of the start of a lesson, made more relevant when they form the basis of further work in the rest of the lesson. Physical warm-ups with the voice are an integral part of any group singing lesson; such exercises can, of course, apply equally to instrumental playing:

Child protection

p. 134 ➤

The whole group, including the teacher, should warm up together using some of the following. Start by focusing on the back, jaw and shoulders, as these areas are particularly susceptible to tension.

- Make funny faces using all the muscles of the face.
- Gently massage the face. Yawn!
- Screw up your face into a ball, then open out into a scream.
- Gently drop the head forward – return to centre – look left and right – return to centre.
- With your fingers, gently tap all over your forehead.
- Imagine you are chewing a piece of sticky toffee except that it starts very small and then gets bigger and bigger inside your mouth. Don't forget to swallow the toffee at the end.
- Poke your tongue out as far as possible and wiggle it about.
- Flop your body forward (like a rag doll) – straighten up slowly.
- Focus on the shoulders by scrunching them up around your ears, then releasing suddenly. Remind the singers that the shoulders should not go up like this when singing.
- Gently roll the shoulders slowly and in large circles – do this exercise with each shoulder separately and then together. Remember to go in both directions.
- Gently massage each other's shoulders.
- Gently wiggle the fingers, then extend this into the arm, then the shoulders – feel floppy and loose.
- Stretch the arms high into the air – stand on tiptoe – hold the balance – lower arms but remain on tiptoe – return to standing flat on the floor.
- Walk about slowly, or on the spot, lifting the knees quite high.   HP

Many of these activities are intended to encourage suppleness of the face and body – an important requirement for singers – and relaxation. They are, of course, also activities that can be used for instrumentalists, since a relaxed body and, in the case of woodwind and brass players, a relaxed face will support good playing. With instrumentalists, the warm-ups can be extended to include activities with the instrument.

Physical warm-ups: clapping games, copycat movement, body percussion. These activities can be led by members of the group as well as the teacher. The clapping and body percussion can get very complicated, with rounds, cross rhythms and improvisation being included. I also do a 'watch me' type exercise in which the pupils have to copy the leader's actions – good for watching the conductor later.

Mouthpiece warm-ups: in a group this can include echo work on rhythmic and melodic patterns, often led by members of the group as well as the teacher. Mini competitions can fit in almost anywhere in the lesson. 'Who can play the longest note?' 'Who can get the highest or lowest on the mouthpiece (not instrument!)?' 'Who has the best posture?', and so on.

Warm-ups on the instrument: these could include long notes, rhythmic and melodic patterns, or work to extend the range. These are a natural extension to the mouthpiece warm-ups and can incorporate elements taken from the physical warm-ups. Once again, leadership can be passed around the group and there is the opportunity for improvisation and composition.

Continuation into work on the instrument but not using written music: chords for intonation; rounds for independence, rhythm and intonation; scales in various guises; introduction of elements from the pieces to be worked on.

Clearly a lot of the above can be done in a one-to-one lesson but I feel that children respond much better to the warm-up games and exercises in a group situation. They are fun as well as being invaluable.   RPr

In the following example, a piano teacher combines singing and playing at the beginning of the lesson.

My preference would be for a brief physical warm-up followed by musicianship skills, technique and then repertoire.

Physical warm-ups: movements away from the keyboard (rolling shoulders, arm swings, and so on) and at the keyboard (sustaining a note with the third finger in each hand and practising flexibility of the wrist in all directions). Encourage pupils to observe possible tension points in each other (knuckles, wrist, elbow, forearm, shoulder, neck) and to think in this way when doing their own practice.

Musicianship skills: aural warm-ups, including Kodály-based ideas that develop aural awareness rather than test it. For example, singing from the root of the scale to each degree in turn (first using letter names or sol-fa, or both, then singing the interval again with its name – thus 'C–D, major 2nd'). It is important to do the same descending from the upper tonic. If pupils are reluctant to sing, don't force them, but go with the flow and let them do it in their own practice if they prefer.

                                                                          MR

Posture

Correct posture and freedom of movement enable pupils to produce a note more easily. The development of a balanced and relaxed posture will, of course, vary from instrument to instrument and teachers will devise different ways to encourage good posture, for example in holding and supporting the instrument comfortably or using the correct grip, sitting and standing while playing and achieving freedom of movement. Again, in a group situation, pupils can help each other:

> All pupils set up on their own and then each is assessed both by the teacher and the other pupils. Individual attention is necessary to get posture and hand positions right. Pupils should check their hand positions before playing so as to develop a precise mental picture of how they work, but be encouraged – from the beginning – not to look while playing.
>
> Posture must be continuously assessed. Relaxation can be encouraged by helping the pupils set up then have them put guitars down, shake their hands loose, walk around the room (if possible) and then set up again independently.   RW/RC
>
> ---
>
> Explore ways of establishing physical freedom by using stretching and relaxing exercises. Ask pupils to consider each other's posture and, if possible, to check their own using a mirror.   HP
>
> ---
>
> Good posture can be reinforced by asking players to check each other. If a whole class is sitting or standing badly and helped to change together, this is often more effective than correcting just one individual.   RPe

Producing a good sound

At every stage of their playing, pupils should be encouraged to make a good sound on their chosen instrument or with their voices. This can be achieved by focusing on a number of aspects of technique, depending on the instrument in question. Things to consider, after breathing (in most cases), are establishing the correct fingering; developing a good embouchure (on woodwind and brass), correct bow-hold (strings) or correct grip for holding sticks or beaters (percussion and steel pans); and, finally, on placing and making the sound. In singing the emphasis is of course on breathing and placing the voice.

Breathing

The physical aspects of breathing can be explained and demonstrated on each other. Make sure that pupils' ribcages expand so that the lungs are filled with air – often this is not the case. Ask them to breathe in slowly through the nose or mouth, making sure that their shoulders do not rise. Then ask them to exhale the air, making sure that they do not physically collapse as the breath runs out.

Placing the voice

Each voice is unique and so care needs to be taken to choose exercises that accommodate everyone. It is preferable to work from high to low. In a group situation it is essential that each voice is cared for individually, so that a high voice has the opportunity to sing high and a low voice can develop the lower notes.   HP

Naturally, breathing is also important preparation for making a sound on an instrument, and the following group exercise for singers could work equally well for instrumentalists.

'Lie on the floor (knees pointing up towards the ceiling) and observe your natural breathing (gentle) – put your hand on your tummy and watch it go up and down – feel your back pushing into the floor.'

'In the standing position, breathe in counting to five – let the air out on a hard "ssss" for ten – relax (let out any leftover air) – do the exercise again, increasing the time of exhalation.' Create a challenge within the group – how far can each member go?

'Breathe in – blow out the air (like blowing out four small candles followed by one very big candle). Put your hand on your diaphragm to feel the movement. Use quick breaths and blow out hard.'

Divide the pupils into two groups at opposite ends of the room. Ask the first group to breathe in quickly and then call out 'hi' to the other group. Make sure that the sound is supported and not a throaty shout. Get the other group to reply in the same manner.

When breathing in it is essential that the abdominal wall is released and relaxed.

Breathing for singing should not be noisy and care should be taken over retaining a relaxed but supported posture.   HP

But the actual making of the sound on an instrument will require attention to a number of other aspects of technique, according to the instrument. In the following examples, two guitar teachers and a piano teacher reflect upon the importance of hand and finger positioning in playing.

Guitar

Dividing early work into thumb melodies (on bass strings), melodies played by alternating fingers (on treble strings), and simple broken-chord textures played by thumb and fingers together (one finger per string) reflects the separate textures and polyphonic strands found in solo guitar music, but allows the necessary techniques to be negotiated separately – not unlike practising separate hands on the piano. Ensemble pieces which initially contain either thumb or finger parts and, later on, alternate between thumb and finger passages within the same part are helpful for this.

It is vital to establish correct hand positions and basic finger and thumb movements from the start. Strong and memorable rhymes and visual images are particularly useful when working with groups. For example:

'Making a fist' replicates the basic movements of the right-hand fingers and thumb. 'Tuck, twist, don't forget the wrist' describes the preparation of the basic right-hand playing position as the hand approaches the strings: the fingers *tuck* under, or fold, from the knuckles into the space behind the thumb. Making sure they stay aligned, the hand and forearm *twist* or rotate slightly, from the elbow, in an anti-clockwise direction ('turn the door-knob' – another image!) so that the fingers point towards the bridge and away from the thumb. 'Don't forget the wrist' refers to making sure the wrist is held at the correct height. This should result in the pupil being able to 'spot the triangle' – the shape made by the thumb, index finger and the line of the strings when the hand is in place ready to play.

And for the left hand, 'Swing, turn, lift, spider'. This comprises letting the left hand fall to the side of the body and swing freely with the shoulder completely relaxed, turning the hand anti-clockwise so that the palm faces forward, lifting the forearm from the elbow, spreading the curved fingers into a spider's leg position and touching the fingerboard where comfortable. 'The rabbit', another example, practises placing the thumb behind the neck correctly in relation to the fingers. The tip of the second finger touches the underside of the thumb tip to make a rabbit's head (the other fingers point upwards). RW/RC

Piano

Scales and arpeggios: I would see teaching these as being as much about musicianship as about technique, but the group situation offers the opportunity to teach a wide range of keys in groups linked by fingering patterns – this can be done by a predominantly aural approach and need not (should not?) be overly influenced by the conventional wisdom of examination requirements.

Piano technique can really be reduced to a relatively small number of fine motor movements, most of which can be easily introduced as larger movements in a group situation. I would certainly encourage teacher demonstration of physical movements followed by some individual practice and then by work in pairs or small groups, looking out for common problems. The extent to which this needs to be teacher-directed would clearly depend upon the nature (age profile, number of pupils, and so on) of the group.

Sensible fingering needs to be promoted from the outset, and is perhaps just as important as suitable physical movements (and is in fact inextricably linked with them). This provides a lot of scope for pupils to take the lead (observing each other's fingering, pointing out good and bad habits, working out fingering patterns in groups or pairs, and so on).

MR

Another example illustrates how pupils can be encouraged, in a group situation, to help each other to find a good hand position.

Woodwind

The pupils can work in pairs to find and develop a good hand position. Pupil A helps pupil B by supporting the weight of the instrument. Next, pupil B places his or her fingers and left-hand thumb in the most effective and comfortable playing position, and then adds the right-hand thumb to see where this is most supportive of the finger position. The thumb should be where it supports the fingers, rather than the fingers moved to suit the thumb. In some cases this may lead to adjustment of the thumb rest. Pupils are not only aware of their own finger position but they understand the reasoning and can continue to help each other.

RPe

The development of a correct embouchure that is suitable and appropriate for the instrument is essential both in woodwind and brass playing.

Woodwind

I show pupils how to check the balance between their embouchure and breath control. I base this on the natural harmonics of the instrument. For the clarinet we all play low A, then add the register key to get E a 12th higher, then remove the left-hand first finger to get C# a 6th higher. If all the notes speak clearly and easily then embouchure and breath control are working well together. A group of three players can try and tune the resulting chord if they play a note each. Players can continue this exercise by moving up in semitone steps as far as a major 3rd.

For flute students we can do this by over-blowing harmonics based on low C and low D.

RPe

And technique does not, of course, have to be taught in isolation from other musical activities.

> New techniques work well when integrated into scale and arpeggio playing, and followed through in the choice of repertoire. It can work well to get everyone to make up a short exercise or piece using, for instance, a new bowing technique or finger pattern. These have to be written down clearly so that everyone in the group can read and play them.
>
> KB

As pupils develop and build the technical skills required to learn to play an instrument or to sing, they will begin to produce a good sound. In the early stages the sound may be erratic, but as they progress they should be able to produce a consistent tone quality, first at a limited dynamic level but later, as they learn a greater number of notes, at a wider dynamic range. At all stages in this process, but especially in a group lesson, they should be taught to listen to the sound they are producing so that they can improve its quality as they master the technical skills.

Intonation

Pupils should be helped and encouraged to play in tune from the outset. This will begin, on some instruments, with learning to tune the instrument correctly, first with guidance from the teacher and later (where appropriate) independently. Pupils should be taught to develop secure intonation and, moreover, to listen to their own and others' playing and adjust their sound as necessary. Intonation will improve if pupils are encouraged to hear and 'sing' each note in their heads before producing it.

> Intonation can be successfully developed by the players just using their clarinet mouthpiece and barrel, on which they should aim to produce a G♯ (concert F♯). With one player keeping a regular G♯ on the complete clarinet, the others have to tune to this. Allow them to experiment with going higher and lower. This really emphasizes the need for listening and adjustment, and it can be applied, with less dramatic results, to the need to listen carefully to intonation when playing. This technique is also useful for checking that the embouchure remains in control when articulation is used. The trick is to tongue in various styles with pitch remaining consistent. Once this is achieved, articulation on the whole instrument should be much improved.
>
> RPe

Articulation

When the combination of preparation, breathing, fingering, embouchure and intonation is secure, the pupil has a good chance of making a pleasing sound when producing or placing the note. Once the sound has been produced, the final stage is to decide how it should be articulated – that is, how the notes and music should be shaped, which of the notes should be separated and which linked to the previous or following notes.

> When teaching the need for accurate and clear articulation, it can be useful to have the group play an articulation pattern together and then have one player play the reverse. For example, the group plays 'slur two, tongue two', one player plays 'tongue two, slur two'. Then discuss the results. It all sounds slurred! RPe

For singers the focus will be on clear diction. For example, the teacher may introduce tongue-twisters and encourage the pupils to make up their own. This technique can also help instrumentalists: the act of verbal articulation helps the recognition and physical articulation of rhythms on the instrument.

> Sing tongue-twisters, such as:
>
> - Margarita, pepperoni, caterpillar, chocolate
> - A proper cup of coffee in a proper copper coffee pot
> - No roses grow on Moses' nose
> - She sits at the window inextricably mimicking him hiccuping but amicably welcoming him in
> - Red lorry, yellow lorry
> - Blackpool pleasure beach
>
> To develop legato singing, the pupils can be asked to sing phrases from songs but take out the consonants, i.e. singing only on the vowels. HP

In conclusion

Technical control of an instrument or voice and an appropriate and developing technique are central to good playing and singing. Wherever possible, the various aspects of technique should be taught within a musical context. Group activities provide good opportunities for pupils to acquire and develop technique with and from each other as well as from the teacher.

Aspects of instrumental technique tend to be specifically developed through the group activities that I use as the basis for the first part of a group lesson, before being applied in the repertoire which the pupils then work on.

Group activities can address fundamental aspects of technique. These are then monitored as I watch and listen to each pupil play. For example, aspects of posture, forearm, wrist and hand positions, naturally curved fingers, fingering techniques, and so forth are all monitored continuously in just the same way that they would be in an individual lesson.

Of course, the larger the group the more diligent the teacher must be in monitoring, because it becomes more difficult to remember which student is struggling with any particular aspect of their physical approach to playing. If I notice that *any* student in the group is developing a bad habit or poor technique in a specific area, I usually introduce a technical exercise for the whole group. This ensures that technical issues are constantly addressed without singling out one pupil for criticism. It also follows that this ensures that all my pupils have a very thorough and secure technical foundation, even though such an exhaustive approach could be said to slow down individual progress. AE

Developing musical skills

Brian Ley

The development of a good technique, which was explored in the last chapter, is a core requirement for instrumentalists and singers, and is therefore a primary activity for instrumental teachers. But there is more to learning to play an instrument than merely acquiring technique. Technical control of an instrument is just a means to an end. So often, though, this 'end' is just playing or singing, and lessons become focused on the practice of pieces. When this happens, pupils simply encounter one piece after another. Yet there is more to being a musician than just acquiring an expanding repertoire of pieces.

Our prime aim as teachers must be to develop pupils' musical understanding through a range of activities that allows them to develop their creative skills as well: to listen purposefully and to explore their own musical ideas, by finding ways of interpreting the music they play or sing, and by improvising and composing. Research cited by Keith Swanwick (*Teaching Music Musically*) confirms the view that pupils need a range of musical experiences and that it would be unwise to base an instrumental curriculum on just playing and the development of performing skills. Our goal must be to nurture and support well-rounded musicians, and give them opportunities to develop their creativity. Good instrumental teaching encourages such active learning: it can occur when both teachers and pupils work creatively. Group work is especially conducive to active learning. Teachers are often able to develop ways of maximizing the whole group's potential for active learning by, for example, allowing and encouraging pupils to take musical risks. This is much easier in a group situation than one-to-one, which can appear to be much more intense.

Listening

Child protection

p. 134 ➡

Listening is fundamental to all musical activity. Encourage your pupils to listen to live and recorded music. Ask them to analyse how the sounds are made, organized and used. Listen to music that is similar in genre and period, and ask them to point out similarities and differences.

Pupils must also be encouraged to listen to and evaluate their own performances. Make regular recordings of your pupils performing so that they can listen to what they are doing. If possible use video, so that they can watch themselves and evaluate their own performances.   HP

I make listening the key sense within the group rather than reading or watching (although these are also important), encouraging students to 'play with the ears rather than with the eyes'. If the participants are playing with what they listen to, there is a chance that they are playing something that can work. It is then for me as the teacher to guide incremental steps forward to a more productive sound.

I emphasize the difference between listening and hearing – listening is a 'doing' activity, hearing is passive. With this message we can introduce listening exercises from time to time. Often this will involve listening 'inside' a backing track (that is, listening intently to particular parts) to understand what is going on.   PC

In instrumental teaching and learning, listening can and should be a creative act, for acquiring good listening skills is an essential part of being a musician. Listening is much more than the aural training which, because of the pressures of time in instrumental lessons, is so often neglected completely or left until the last few weeks before an examination. Aural skills can be developed as part of the broader listening experience. Such broader experience will include, for example, listening to live and recorded music. This could perhaps form the focus of a lesson or series of lessons to develop an appreciation of how sounds are made and organized, so that pupils might better reflect upon and understand how these sounds are used in the pieces they play.

Listening games for younger players can keep them focused and help develop aural awareness. 'Spot the deliberate mistake' is a favourite. The teacher will play a short section of a piece incorporating a deliberate mistake and get everyone to follow the music and find it. If appropriate, each child in the group can take it in turns to do their own 'mistake'.   KB

...Spot the deliberate mistake...

Listening in performance should also be encouraged, to help pupils improve and refine their skills – their intonation for example – and to focus their awareness on interpretation. Listening is also obviously central to the skill of improvisation.

I encourage pupils to listen by:

- copying both the teacher and each other;
- working on intonation and togetherness within the group and individually;
- working on awareness: questioning about what just happened in a piece is often very interesting – this is much easier to develop in a group situation;
- teacher modelling and demonstration;
- giving suggestions for wider listening: CDs, concerts, radio, TV, etc.;
- getting them to use information and communication technology (ICT) to record and listen to their own performances. RPr

The group situation is ideal for encouraging everyone to listen. Presenting a wide range of repertoire for pupils to choose pieces will also require them to listen to different styles, and this can be linked to some basic stylistic knowledge. With older pupils a listening project could be useful – one in which they give a very short presentation on a piece (possibly from a list provided) that they have listened to. Keeping a record of repertoire that has been studied and a list of repertoire listened to could also encourage a range of stylistic awareness. MR

In some instrumental disciplines, such as steel pans, listening is absolutely essential to the way the music is learnt.

> The teaching of steel pans is unusual in that it does not typically follow the format of traditional music-teaching in this country. The approach is nearly always practical and sheet music is rarely used. Players learn melodies, chords, harmonies and bass-lines by listening and then playing them from memory.　　　　TC

The examples above illustrate that listening is much more than just hearing a piece or following verbal instructions. In group work, the teacher can engage the pupils through specifically directed listening activities.

> Listening has to do with focus, whether we mean listening to music or concentrating on talking and instructions. I find that the pupils' focus needs to be *directed* by the teacher; otherwise their minds tend to wander. Simple directions usually empower pupils to engage far more effectively in listening.
>
> So, for example, if one player in the group is performing to the others, I will usually give the rest of the group something particular to listen out for, and then follow up the performance with questions to the others (as well as to the player). Without seeming contrived, such direction is usually effective in helping all the members of the group to stay engaged with the music even when others are playing.　　　　AE

Pupils' understanding of what they are listening to is enhanced when, in the early stages of their playing, they are able to talk about the music. As they progress, they can begin to analyse, compare and evaluate the music that they have made or been listening to – in other words, they are enabled to appraise the music. Appraising makes the listening process more intelligible.

Listening and appraising are essential to group teaching. In the group situation, pupils can be encouraged to share their listening experiences and to help and support each other in appraising their work.

> There are many opportunities to listen in the group lesson; if an individual is playing it is good to focus the others' attention on a particular point and invite comment. This constant appraisal of each other feeds into their own playing and seems to heighten awareness.
>
> Group tuition offers extra pairs of ears. There is a larger pool of information to draw

from. Pupils can listen to and comment upon each other's performance as well as their own. This is an easier introduction to self-assessment than trying to perform and assess at the same time. Students are normally encouraged to think forwards, but a listener can retain comment.

Keep asking them what they have heard. They should comment on balance, intonation, character, notes (are they correct?), rhythm, maintenance of pulse, dynamic range, and articulation – in fact every element they have been taught to consider. As a general rule, get comments from the pupils before adding any of your own.

If there are things they have missed, I may play to them what I heard and if necessary play what I should have heard. Can they spot the difference?   RPe

Critical peer appraisal is often much more positive than self-appraisal. Many children seem unwilling to pick out the good bits of their own performance, but are much more generous when giving a critique of a friend's. One way of developing this is to set up an expectation that the first thing one mentions about a performance is always positive.   RPr

Playing and interpreting pieces

Pupils will, of course, play pieces of music and build up a repertoire as they progress in their lessons. Pupils' creativity in their playing and singing can also be developed from the early stages as fluency and expression gradually evolve in their rendering of simple pieces. As they advance, and they tackle more difficult pieces in a wider range of styles, their understanding will grow too, and as a result they will be able to communicate the character of the music. In the more advanced stages, pupils will bring their own ideas to the interpretation of the music they play.

All music has to be played with an appropriate sense of style and an awareness of period conventions. With the privilege of instrumental lessons, pupils can achieve the 'excellent performance' assessment criteria of the National Curriculum – that is: they can discriminate and develop different interpretations; they can express their own ideas and feelings in a developing personal style, exploiting instrumental possibilities; they can give convincing performances and demonstrate empathy with other performers; and they can also discriminate and comment on how and why changes occur within selected traditions of performance and composition.   RPe

Musical interpretation involves pupils making decisions, from the start, about the pieces they play. This may mean their talking about the music and discussing how it might be played – considering, for example, tempo, dynamics and effective phrasing. In group lessons, pupils may be encouraged to discuss their ideas for interpretation with each other and the teacher, to develop their own interpretative strategies. For example, they could listen to each other's playing and appraise each other's performance, making suitable suggestions for future performances. As confidence grows, so pupils may begin to make different choices when interpreting pieces (solo or ensemble), thereby 'making the music their own'. The group lesson provides an ideal situation for pupils, at any stage in their playing, to develop their interpretative skills through discussion and through listening to and appraising each other's playing. Furthermore, playing pieces by ear, from memory and at sight, while developing interpretative skills, improves pupils' aural awareness and their all-round musicianship.

Improvising

The value of improvisation is enormous. In the very early stages improvisation can be encouraged simultaneously in two ways. The first is the exploration of sound colours and effects with no particular structural framework, possibly initiated by pictorial images. The second is danger-free improvisation within particular constraints. For the latter, modes or pentatonic scales are useful – anything that gets away from semitones and the concept of 'wrongness'. Pentatonic scales are absolutely ideal in group keyboard lessons because the black keys allow for easily identifiable 'major' and 'minor' pentatonics, and even a group pentatonic improvisation – given the framework of a metrical pulse and tempo – can work very well. MR

8

**Improvising
and composing**

Improvising is perhaps one of the most creative of musical activities and one which can not only inform pupils' playing but also improve their other musical skills, as Harris and Crozier identify:

There are a number of reasons why a young player might spend part of a lesson or practice session improvising. These include:

- improving aural skills;
- improving technical skills;
- increasing general musical awareness;
- developing confidence;
- exploring the instrument;
- exploring music without notation;
- cultivating self-expression;

- developing skills required in certain exams;
- developing a facility in a particular musical genre;
- developing the inner ear and the ability to think ahead musically.

(Harris and Crozier, *The Music Teacher's Companion*, p. 68)

Improvisation is often associated with jazz, but this is just one area in which these skills can be developed. Improvising is central to many other types of music in the Western tradition (including pop and folk) as well as in music of other cultures. Improvisation is best practised with others and is therefore an ideal vehicle for group teaching.

> I introduce improvisation through echo games at a very early stage (lesson one): teacher leads and pupils respond. Later I extend this to pupils leading. Then I introduce the concept of question and answer as an extension to the echo, add a harmonic underpinning and away you go, developing as the pupils improve. In the group lesson the advantages are support from the group; the opportunity to move on all the time so the pupils don't feel trapped; and the ability to add harmony from others in the group rather than from an external source. This appears simplistic and easier said than done, I know, but the important thing is to introduce improvisation early, keep it simple and make success inevitable. Once again, the 'safety' of a group situation makes this easier, I feel.   RPr
>
> Ask pupils to recognize dynamic, articulation and tempo changes in a piece played by the teacher. Play to the pupils to demonstrate changes of colour, musical character or style. Ask some pupils to play a simple four-bar phrase with their own spontaneous interpretative ideas while the others describe what happened.   RW/RC

Improvisation forms a natural part of a group singing lesson. In the following example, the act of improvising is integral to the study of pieces, illustrating a holistic approach to teaching and learning. This type of activity would, of course, work equally well in an instrumental lesson.

> An easy start into improvisation – the teacher sings a short phrase which the pupils complete by singing the final note.
>
> Ask a pupil to sing a short improvised phrase. Then ask the next pupil to carry on with an answering phrase starting on the final note of the previous one.
>
> Identify some interesting rhythmic patterns from a familiar song and improvise a rhythmic sequence based on these patterns. Alternatively, devise an ostinato pattern

to fit a song being studied – some members of the group sing the song while others perform the ostinato. The ultimate aim is to try and do both song and ostinato at the same time.

Introduce pupils to different scales and modes, and encourage experimentation with them. Easy access into the Dorian mode could be through 'What shall we do with the drunken sailor?' or 'Scarborough Fair'. Pupils could also devise some call-and-response exercises in the Dorian mode.

Take the basic chord structure of a song being studied and encourage pupils to improvise their own melody over it.

Always encourage and praise improvisation, however small and short the improvisation might be. Some pupils thrive on being free to go off on their own. Others find it terrifying. All should be encouraged.   HP

When improvising, pupils often play music that is both more technically advanced than what they meet playing written music, and more complex in its language. For example, pupils might effectively improvise in compound time before they have been introduced to compound time-signatures or fully understood the concept of dividing the beat into three subdivisions. Improvisation is therefore not only worthwhile in its own right but it is a useful vehicle for introducing other technical and musical aspects of playing.   AE

There are, therefore, a number of approaches to improvisation – using musical patterns, scales and modes, and developing ideas from existing material, such as the songs or repertoire being studied. Whatever the approach, perhaps the main point is that improvisation engages pupils directly with the sound itself.

Composing

8

Improvising and composing

Since the introduction of the National Curriculum, composing has become a common feature of the general music classroom experience. Composing also plays an important role in instrumental tuition, not only in its own right to further develop pupils' creative skills but as an activity that can complement and support the development of other musical skills, such as performing and interpretation. Composing can follow on naturally from improvising. Arranging forms an important strand of the composing process and for many pupils – especially in the intermediate and more advanced stages of learning – the ability to arrange a piece of music, say for the combination of instruments within the group lesson or for an out-of-school ensemble, complements composing. Composing and arranging can also fulfil the requirements for examinations such as GCSE and AS/A level, and as such form a natural link between classroom and instrumental music.

> Improvising call-and-response, and using rondo shapes (teacher plays the rondo, pupils play episodes), can provide a useful starting point for the composition phase, and can help to reinforce understanding of form in pieces. Equally repertoire, for example pieces in ternary form, can be useful as a model for pupils' compositions. In the very early stages a simple piece could be turned into a ternary piece by using a B section composed by the pupil, helping to reinforce concepts of unity and contrast.
>
> MR

Composing is sometimes regarded as an activity that can be undertaken away from the lesson, best related to a classroom music experience rather than a group instrumental lesson. But many instrumental teachers recognize the value that their pupils gain not only from making up their own music and improvising around given notes, a theme or in a particular style, but also in the developing and structuring of their work, more formally, into a composition. Compositions can often grow from improvisations and will sometimes form the basis for homework.

> This can be an extension and formalization of the improvisation or a separate activity. Group composition work can include discussion and take place very early on. A group I teach 'composed' a tune after only a few weeks' tuition and knowing only three notes. We had a discussion about what note we should start and end on, what the shape should be, devised a graphic score (whiteboards are wonderful things!), sang it and then played it.
>
> Later on, the group can be used to perform compositions made by individual members and useful discussion can be generated on what works, or doesn't, and how the piece can be developed.   RPr

Composing, then, can not only grow from improvisation but it can be tackled well in groups.

> Pupils remember their improvisations and recall them as 'pieces' or parts of pieces. Individual ideas can be brought together in a group composition. From there it is a short step to using manuscript paper to store the ideas. By using notes they are familiar with, they will know what they look like and enjoy writing them out themselves, using printed examples as a reference.   RW/RC

Choose a memorable phrase from a song being learnt. Ask the pupils to compose a short song based on that phrase.

More advanced pupils may wish to try and compose a short unaccompanied piece for the voices in the group. This could be with or without words. Encourage pupils to use devices such as repetition or sequence and incorporate some dynamic variations. They could record their work on tape or write it down using conventional or pattern notation.

HP

Furthermore, improvisation and composition can be developed almost simultaneously.

At an early stage, improvising may lead on to composing. Where pupils have developed really good ideas through improvising I encourage them to repeat those ideas and commit them to memory, perhaps also recording them into the keyboard using the onboard sequencer if it has one. As their knowledge of staff notation develops they can also begin to use this as a means of remembering musical ideas. Where appropriate I correct the theoretical aspect of their notation, and give advice on developing compositions further. I should stress, however, that it is only a minority of pupils who develop an interest in composition at this stage.

With more advanced pupils I often find that they want to show me – and the other members of their group – the compositions that they have done in the classroom as part of (for example) their GCSE coursework. Once again I see my role as encouraging their creativity and, where appropriate, offering advice, particularly with regard to instrumental technique.

I feel that I must be careful not to duplicate the work of my classroom colleagues. My work as an instrumental teacher is within the context of a wider team of professionals who contribute together to the pupils' overall musical development. Perhaps the most important benefit of teaching an instrument within the school is to provide a 'joined up' approach to music teaching, working co-operatively with the school.

AE

It is important to note, in this last quotation, the importance of the whole music-education programme that many pupils study in schools – classroom music, instrumental lessons and extra- and extended-curricular activities. Composing is not the sole preserve of the classroom teacher; neither are aspects of instrumental teaching – especially ensemble skills – the sole domain of the instrumental teacher. Good classroom and instrumental teachers (both private and those working in schools) appreciate the need, wherever possible, to work together in pursuit of the common goal of providing rich musical experiences for their pupils.

In conclusion

The technical skills of playing an instrument and of singing form the basis of instrumental teaching and learning. But in order for pupils to become effective all-round musicians, their technique needs to underpin and support the development of other essential musical skills – listening and appraising, performing, improvising and composing. Group teaching provides opportunities for pupils to develop these musicianship skills in ways that are mutually supportive. It also encourages both pupils and teachers to work creatively.

5

Developing ensemble skills

Brian Ley

> Make performance a natural part of playing. It is much less intimidating in a group than solo playing and many players have no wish to be soloists; they get their pleasure from playing and making music in a team situation. RPr

When pupils learn to play a musical instrument, whether in group lessons or in one-to-one tuition, they will engage in a number of activities that will support and promote their whole musical learning. They will develop technical control of their instrument and they will listen, applying the skills they have learnt to both singing and playing pieces and to improvising and composing. But the lesson alone provides only part of the rich musical experience that is learning to play an instrument. From the early stages occasions should be made available for pupils to perform. For groups, the weekly lesson will, of course, provide opportunities for them to play to their teacher and to each other, and this is a vitally important aspect of ensemble work. The group lesson will provide the anchor for the development of ensemble skills if the teacher provides activities that enable pupils to listen, watch, react and communicate, and to blend the sounds they make on their instruments.

Performing to a wider audience is a natural extension of the instrumental learning process. The performances could be part of informal presentations such as to school assembly or to friends, but they can include formal occasions such as festivals, concerts, recitals as part of examinations, and so on. This type of performing reinforces and extends the skills that the pupils have acquired in their lessons; it often has the effect of 'bringing their playing to life'. Opportunities are sometimes available for many pupils to join together in ensemble in school choirs, orchestras and bands. In addition, almost all LEA Music Services run local music centres (where pupils often receive their first ensemble experience), area orchestras and bands, choirs, steel pan and drumming and percussion groups.

Performing skills need to be taught and performance must be prepared, so how?

Beginning ensemble work

Even in the early stages of group work pupils can and should be encouraged to play or sing to and with each other, so that they begin to develop ensemble skills.

> Start in lesson one by doing things together, as the whole essence of ensemble skill is the awareness of others and keeping together. One of the sayings I really hate is the old one of 'you can't join an ensemble until you reach "x" standard', often said by teachers of individuals. Pupils *can* work together from the beginning and should be encouraged to join larger ensembles (carefully constructed to be positive, enjoyable experiences) as soon as possible.   RPr

Being aware of others in a group and keeping together in ensemble involves the pupils listening, watching and responding to both the conductor, or director, and each other. These skills can be developed initially in the group lesson through games and activities such as echoing, 'follow my leader', and rounds (where pupils take individual parts), as well as by playing simple chord progressions to improve accuracy of pitch and togetherness.

> It is easier for beginner string groups to play in unison at first but the skills needed for ensemble playing can be introduced from the earliest stages. Here are a few of the ideas which I use.
>
> - The group will play a simple open string part, by ear (probably just the D and A strings to begin with), to simple traditional tunes such as 'Lightly Row'. Ask them to listen and work out when to change to the next note – this develops an awareness of harmonic changes. Tunes which can be harmonized with three notes are then introduced.
> - Always do homorhythmic material at first and get the whole group playing the easy part while the teacher plays the 'harder' part. This will help with rhythmic security. If the material is not homorhythmic, the teacher should try to bow in the same direction as the rest of the group to give encouragement.
> - Ensemble material should be about a grade easier than the group has actually achieved.

- Playing scales and arpeggios as rounds is valuable ensemble practice as well as helping with intonation.
- Practising beginnings and endings, even with a unison piece, is worth doing. Nominate someone in the group to be the leader and make them responsible for bringing everyone in at the start and off at the end. This develops awareness of others in the group and encourages everyone to watch and listen. The layout of the stands is important so that eye contact can be made; this is not always practical in some teaching rooms! The techniques needed for starting and ending have to be taught and practised often – every lesson! And ensure that everyone gets a turn.
- Pulse and rhythm games can be used to develop ensemble skills. One player taps the pulse, the others the rhythm of their part. Or everyone can play for four bars, stop for two bars, then start again. This can heighten awareness of keeping a steady pulse.
- To develop understanding of balance within an ensemble, pupils need to be aware of the concepts of melody and accompaniment; exaggerating dynamics can be useful at first.

                                                                                          KB

The development of ensemble skills applies equally well, of course, in the group singing lesson as in the instrumental lesson. Many of the skills and approaches outlined in the following example, designed for singers, would apply equally well to instrumentalists.

- Make sure that the pupils have an opportunity to sing individually as well as in the group. As the teacher you need to keep an eye on everyone's development.
- Ask the pupils to sing different parts within a vocal piece so that they understand how the whole piece fits together and know which part is the most significant.
- For each piece, encourage a different leader who will be responsible for bringing everyone in (in the case of an unaccompanied piece), conducting, choosing the speed or suggesting dynamics.
- Remind the singers to listen to each other 'sideways' when they are singing, and make sure that the lowest voice is not always stuck on the bottom part or the highest voice on the top part. Vary the parts and the voices.
- Use rounds – this is an easy and effective way of singing in parts quickly and impressively!
- If there are four singers in the group, start with a two-part piece (two voices to a part) so that it can be performed well and with confidence. Change arrangements so that each person takes a solo line at unison points.
- Use a variety of music – don't get stuck in one particular genre. Begin with a style that is liked by all, but later on try out something different.

                                                                                          HP

Ensemble skills can also be developed effectively in group piano teaching.

In the first instance, some of the activities suitable for sight-reading (some members of the class maintaining a pulse, others reading rhythms, etc.) are a good springboard for ensemble activities. So are any of the aural or improvisation activities, in that they encourage listening, teamwork and sensitivity. It is also worth pointing out that there is a vast amount of four- , six- and, to a lesser extent, eight-hand repertoire available to pianists. Nadia Lasserson's book *The Piano Needn't be Lonely* is a good source of information. The resources of the Keyboard Lab can be effectively applied in this area, because with a reasonably sophisticated set-up, pairs of pupils can 'tune in' to each other without being heard by the rest of the class. Multi-keyboard repertoire is also possible, though the idea of more than one person to a part does not usually occur to piano teachers and can make a fairly fearsome racket (though recently at the RNCM we had a piece written for an education outreach project which was played by thirty-six pianists of varying ages and abilities).

Teachers should consider using repertoire which is well within the capabilities of the players so that the ensemble experience is a positive one rather than a struggle. Also, it is obviously a good idea to ensure that each of the players knows the music fairly well in advance of any rehearsals. MR

It is important to note that playing in an ensemble makes particular demands on young players and needs a special set of skills: holding their own line while others are playing other parts; staying in time and tune with others; listening and blending; watching and reacting; and being conscious of their contribution to the whole. These skills will be best developed if pupils are not also struggling with technical, rhythmic or musical problems in their own parts. Many of the teacher-contributors make the point that ensemble repertoire needs to be well within the technical and musical range of the individual players. This is so that pupils feel comfortable with what they themselves are playing while learning to play with others.

Playing together

When training other teachers to start keyboard ensembles I outline some of the most important considerations for keyboard ensemble playing:

Conduct
- Respect one another and listen to the group leader.
- Don't doodle! Play only when required.

- Discuss as a group how choices of voice, auto-accompaniment, and so on affect the balance and character of the music.
- Be sensible when setting up and taking apart equipment.
- Rehearsals are more enjoyable and rewarding if you take them seriously.

Watching

- Can I make eye contact with all the other players?
- What signals can we use?
- How does the piece start?
- How does the piece end?
- How presentable are we? Will we look good in front of an audience?

Choosing voices

Ask:

- What style of music are we playing, and what voices generally suit this style?
- Which part has the tune?
- Which voice is suitable for my part? (consider articulation, volume)
- Am I loud enough?
- Am I too loud?
- Can I hear all the other parts clearly?
- Are other players in the group too loud or not loud enough?

Listening

- Are we in time with each other and with the auto-accompaniment?
- Is the balance good?
- Does our choice of registration improve the music?
- What cues in the music can I listen out for?

These points are simply those that any ensemble will continuously revisit during its rehearsal and development. In the same way that important aspects of technique and musicianship will continuously be assessed and revisited as part of the ongoing tuition during lessons, these elements of ensemble playing will always need to be in the mind of a teacher who rehearses keyboard ensembles. AE

The role of the director

Performing in a group is much more than just playing the right notes in the right order, however important that may be. A musical performance involves the performers being aware of the mood and style of the music and being able to convey this together in their ensemble playing. The role of the director – who is often, appropriately, the instrumental teacher – is not merely to ensure that the right technique is used to play

...Am I too loud?...

the notes correctly; it is also crucial in helping pupils to learn to interpret the character of the music. It is also about developing within pupils a sense of musical understanding through performance in a way which engages them fully in the creative process of making and sharing music.

Firstly, take great care to choose appropriate music. The pieces must be accessible by all the players, so a musical result can be achieved fairly quickly. All the parts should be interesting, important and have the tune at some point. The music should have 'quality', i.e. is it worth playing and will the pupils be proud to perform it?

Make the players aware of the fact that they have to help each other and how they can help. An accompanying section must be aware of which player has the melody, and balance and support accordingly. The melody player must achieve a solo sound and be very clear, especially if there is any rubato involved. RPe

The director's role is also one of keeping the ensemble together.

The teacher must establish the 'ground rules' of ensemble playing, such as:

- no one plays until told to;
- hands ready in position;
- look at the teacher;
- listen to instructions (for example, 'We are starting at bar 5').

Pupils learn they have a responsibility to their peers, so that if they lose their place they not only let themselves down but the whole ensemble. RW/RC

Bear in mind that, on occasions, pupils will benefit hugely from directing the group themselves and from taking personal responsibility for the performance. Individual pupils could be encouraged to direct or, in the case of a small ensemble, to lead the group. This would mean ensuring that the rest of the group is ready to play, and counting in correctly and maintaining eye contact with the rest of the players to ensure that the ensemble is together. When pupils are given autonomy in this way, it has a profoundly beneficial effect on their self-confidence. More advanced pupils may be encouraged to make interpretative decisions about how the group should play; to reflect on the group's performance and assess its good and bad points; and to diagnose problems within the ensemble and suggest remedies for them.

Performing to an audience

Awareness of an audience, the venue and the occasion itself are all important aspects of effective performance. Occasions such as a public presentation more often than not lift musical standards and enhance pupils' enjoyment of playing. An essential element of performance is the ability of the performers to communicate. In other words, players need to convey the spirit or meaning of the music – and their understanding of it – to their listeners. In order to communicate effectively with an audience, pupils might be encouraged to think about the meaning of the music from the outset, by being asked:

- What is going on in the music?
- How is the music structured?
- How should we play each section?
- What should be contrasted?
- What is the background to the piece?
- What do you think the composer intends in this piece?

During rehearsals, especially those shortly before the performance, when the pupils are more confident about their playing, the teacher could discuss various aspects of the performance they are about to give. For example, as well as discussing the technical and expressive elements, such as how to start the piece (by watching the conductor) or at what dynamic level to begin, the group could discuss dress code, or how to walk on and off the performance area and how to acknowledge the applause at the end. Encouraging group members to share their individual anticipations of the event can be useful in other ways. Teachers may well find that enthusiasm is infectious, generating energy for the performance. On the other hand, any nervousness that pupils express about playing in public is likely to be diffused if shared by the group. Pupils should recognize that performance 'nerves' are a natural phenomenon for amateur and professional musicians alike.

After a performance, they should be encouraged to consider:

- How well do you think we played?
- What could we improve for the next performance?

> In the lesson following the concert, don't forget to discuss the performances – positive and negative issues. Ask pupils how they thought it went. Try to encourage them to be open and realistic about their evaluation – so often pupils will say 'Oh, it was terrible', or 'It was OK'. Get them to really break down what was good and what could do with some improvement.
>
> HP

Opportunities for performance

Public performance, in front of any audience, is an important milestone for any musician, but especially for the young. There are many opportunities for performance, in school as well as outside. They may include:

> - playing to other groups having lessons (easy to do as the groups change over, for example: 'Listen to what we have been working on in this lesson – what do you think?');
> - playing to a class in the school (involve the school in planning);
> - inviting parents into a lesson at the end of term (check with the school first);
> - playing in assembly (talk well in advance to the head or teacher responsible);
> - taking part in the school concert or open day (again, discuss this with the relevant teachers);
> - taking part in local music-centre concerts, both as part of the larger band and also playing solos or small-group items;
> - taking a band 'on tour' to other schools;
> - holding a concert of one's own pupils (or sharing one with one or two other teachers).
>
> RPr

Many of these performance opportunities stem from the experience that pupils gain during lessons. Activities that are integral to group work can extend beyond the group lesson, in circumstances where larger groups of more varied abilities can come together and learn from each other. This peer support is beneficial because more advanced players can act as 'leaders' and support others in the group, while less experienced players will often 'lift' their performance when playing alongside better players. Pupils may also have the chance to play in mixed ensembles – such as orchestras or bands – as well as in ensembles of the same instrument.

Woodwind

Performance opportunities are many. Some are carefully planned and some impromptu. Planned performances can include playing in front of the class (if group members are in the same class), playing for major school concerts, creating a small informal presentation for parents, playing at school assemblies, playing at local schools, playing at old peoples' homes, and busking in the city as part of a school project. Impromptu performances can be one group playing to the next group or the two groups playing together.

As their teacher I would encourage students to perform and make sure they can do so with confidence. I am usually there to support them but some school functions I am unable to attend. As long as the group is well rehearsed and they understand how to relate to each other they are fine. Afterwards I will congratulate them (if I was there) or ask them how it went if I was not.

RPe

Keyboard

Specific events that I organize for keyboard players include a regular informal keyboard concert once a term (including solo and ensemble items) and a large keyboard 'spectacular' every one to two years (ensembles only). I also organize an informal piano recital once or twice a term and a formal piano recital every summer, as well as hosting the occasional masterclass for our piano students.

I try to encourage all the schools where I teach to give plenty of performance opportunities to my pupils. Most of the schools I work with have at least one public concert a year, as well as giving opportunities for players to perform in school assemblies. At the largest school I teach in, I have formed a lunchtime 'keyband', which has begun to perform more widely, including playing at the Education Fair at the National Exhibition Centre in Birmingham earlier this year.

In all cases I try to be present when my pupils are performing. I see public performance as a particular goal of my teaching, and believe that my support on the day is highly important to my students. It is also important that I give assistance at a practical level to these electronic keyboard players, because of the difficult logistics of setting up electrical and PA equipment – often in a confined performing space – with due care and attention to health and safety issues.

Lastly, in the case of many of the ensemble performances, I take part as a conductor in the performance. Even where this is unnecessary (because the group has good visual communication and the auto-accompaniment provides a steady pulse) I have found that the presence of a conductor is visually beneficial for the audience, helping them to understand which player is performing which part of the music.

AE

Singing

I arrange regular pupils' concerts so that they become used to performing. This helps their overall confidence and development. Give the pupils plenty of notice and preparation time – don't spring a concert on them. Make sure they are at their best so that they can perform to their greatest potential. Invite parents and friends – make it a special occasion by having a tea afterwards. Ask a group member to design a poster. Prepare a printed programme. Make it an important occasion and pupils will rise to the challenge. Ask them to introduce their songs – practise this in the lesson. If possible, accompany your pupils on the piano or other instrument. If this is not possible, arrange to use another pianist, but make sure they have a rehearsal together before the concert, so that they both know what they are doing. Alternatively, use backing tracks. Always be encouraging after the concert; everyone who has performed has succeeded in some way.   HP

Piano

Performances within the lesson can be a regular feature and indeed can provide a welcome opportunity for parental involvement. Other than that, informal opportunities within the school (particularly seasonal ones like Christmas) are helpful – pianists are lucky in that they can perform alone or as part of a duet or other ensemble. As pupils grow in confidence, they can be offered opportunities to announce their pieces and say something about them. Involvement before performances will obviously include making sure that pieces are thoroughly learnt, giving try-outs in the lesson, dealing with taking a bow, and so on. Discussion after performances is often overlooked, but it can be very enlightening, and perhaps becomes increasingly important as the pupil becomes more advanced.   MR

Strings

All pupils are encouraged to join a larger ensemble group or orchestra to provide further performance opportunities. I am involved in running most of the larger groups that my students attend, so this can reinforce work done in the lesson. It gives a positive message to pupils if their teacher attends a concert that they are taking part in and it can be useful to discuss and follow up the concert during lessons. For older students, helping with the 'tricky bit' in their orchestra music is important. Likewise, lending them a CD of a piece they are doing in youth orchestra gives the message that you are interested in all that they are involved with.

Younger players are usually given a sticker for playing in assembly and these informal opportunities to perform are very beneficial and help build their confidence.   KB

These examples all illustrate the variety of performance opportunities in various instrumental disciplines, and many of them would equally apply to mixed instrumental ensembles. The following example, however, illustrates a very important aspect of ensemble playing: the possibility of pupils organizing and directing their own performances. Intermediate and more advanced players, particularly, can gain much from playing in small ensembles where they have to rely upon their own musical judgements and skills in presenting, starting, playing together and ending a piece. Their musical skills, knowledge and understanding can be greatly enhanced through developing independence in their performing.

Percussion

Wherever possible, I encourage the group or ensemble to be self-sufficient. This way members develop qualities of leadership and self-motivation and, most importantly, awareness of the possibility that performance can happen without me around. I encourage the possibility of impromptu performance, and therefore attempt to break down the barriers to performance which are created each time instruments have to be set up and placed, music found and stands set up, a hall unlocked and an ensemble layout reworked. Consider the advantages of working without written music, and of having simple instruments within the ensemble easily accessible. Try to find a space where the ensemble set-up can remain reasonably intact. These are significant difficulties to overcome, but once established will allow many more performance opportunities.

One problem with public performance is that the percussion ensemble sometimes becomes the novelty item within the programme. Of course there is a time and place for this, but all too often it is the expectation. Try to present the percussion ensemble as a musically valid grouping, not just to the audience but also (possibly more importantly) to your peers and professional colleagues at the school. These people can be considered stakeholders in the future direction of your percussion department.

With any percussion group there are always logistical issues. These will always be offered up as reasons why there should not be a percussion ensemble performance. Think through all possible ways to reduce the logistical inconvenience and the awkward pauses that occur in a concert when percussionists have to reorganize large amounts of equipment. Percussion can often be very effective when it is small, quiet and short.

PC

In conclusion

There is more to music-making than what happens between 9.00 a.m. and 3.30 p.m. in the classroom, in instrumental lessons or, for that matter, within the confines of the private music studio. Learning to play together in a group lesson is an important step in developing core musical skills. Good group teaching *is* teaching in ensemble. Performing in ensembles (of mixed or similar instruments and of mixed or similar ability) is a natural extension to the weekly lesson; it helps to develop all sorts of social and other benefits as well as skills of performance and communication. Above all, it brings a fresh and often exciting dimension to pupils' overall musical experience.

Because, it is hoped, initial experiences of small group and ensemble playing have been a natural and enjoyable part of the lessons, it becomes easier to persuade pupils to join larger ensembles at school or local music centres. I find that, once I have got to this stage, drop out is very low for the first three to four years (when the adolescent bit kicks in!). RPr

6

Encouraging progress

Brian Ley

As committed instrumental teachers – whoever we work with, in whatever circumstances and at whatever level – we want our pupils to succeed musically. Our role is to encourage them to progress as well as they can so that they achieve well and attain the highest standards they are capable of reaching.

We usually use the term 'standards' to mean the musical attainment of pupils in relation to clear, externally organized criteria such as graded examinations. And we tend to use these criteria as common currency when judging ability or skill level. For example, when we say a pupil is 'about Grade 3', we usually know the examination requirements on that particular instrument and are able to judge the pupil against these. In fact we tend to use these terms fairly frequently. But that information does not tell the whole story about how well our pupils are doing. For example, consider a pupil who, within three years of starting to learn an instrument, attains Grade 4 at the age of 10. We may say not only that this pupil has reached a high standard of playing but also that, given his or her age and the length of time learning, he or she is making good (if not excellent) progress and achieving well. On the other hand, a pupil of the same age who has been learning for three years and has still to attain Grade 1 may be regarded as making slower progress, though because of particular social or other background factors he or she may be achieving as well as can be expected, and may nevertheless enjoy and benefit from music lessons.

Musical standards, musical achievement and progress are therefore separate though related terms. To judge how well pupils are doing we need to consider their personal circumstances, the progress they have made over the period of time they have been learning and also the level of demand made of them. Good teaching enables pupils to make good progress at any level, whatever their circumstances. One of the challenges in group teaching is to make sure that all pupils progress as well as they can in an environment where their abilities and background may vary. This is possible when teachers motivate all the pupils equally, and when they take account of and build upon the ability of each group member, providing suitable challenges for each one of them.

Motivating pupils

Motivation is crucial to pupils' learning for it will determine how much they enjoy playing or singing and how effectively they learn. Motivation can be intrinsic, coming from within each pupil, but motivation can also be influenced, extrinsically, by the actions of the teacher or from other members of the group.

Motivation

p. 108 →

Personally, I find motivation much easier in group lessons. During a pupil's development there are swings between intrinsic and extrinsic motivation. At the beginning there is the initial rush of intrinsic motivation caused by a (frequently ill-defined) wish to play something. This is very often complicated by parental or other external pressure on the choice of instrument (on account of money, size, needs of the school band, availability of instruments, parental ambition, parents living through their children, etc.). After this first 'golden period' there is the terrible realization that work (hard grind) is needed for satisfactory development and this is where the need for teacher and peer support really kicks in. There is also the point when all children go through some sort of adolescent period and other issues in their life take on a greater importance. Sometimes, of course, having learnt an instrument for some years, they decide it is time to do something else – and I do not think that this should necessarily be regarded as a failure.

Where the group situation really helps is in keeping that initial enthusiasm going for much longer. Peer and adult pressure can be a destructive force in schools (negative comments about carrying instrument cases on the bus, having to come out of academic lessons, and so on); so having others to share the experience is very important. Belonging to a group rather than being an individual can be a tremendous help. Understanding progress and problems can be handled more supportively in groups. A pupil can measure their progress against others (so it is important that the teacher finds something positive to highlight for all pupils in a session) and it can be encouraging for a pupil to see others having similar problems – they can understand that it is a normal part of learning and not their individual failure.

RPr

Peer support and challenge are very important factors in good group teaching. So often, when working in groups, it is the pupils themselves who motivate each other.

> Motivation is usually self-generating in group teaching. Pupils see what their colleagues are doing and often try harder as a result of the natural competitiveness that is generated.   RW/RC

Musical challenges

While we would all hope and expect that our pupils will become self-motivated and be able to work independently between lessons, the teacher will often need to provide the additional motivation that will prompt pupils to work harder and to progress well in their playing. This can be achieved when they are challenged musically and when sufficient (but not too severe) musical demands are made of them. Pupils generally respond well when we set realistic challenges for them. If we agree targets with them, for example over a period of a half-term, this can not only provide a challenge to all but can also lead to competition within the group. Used skilfully, this can have an energizing effect on pupils.

> Group teaching can carry along a reluctant member who perhaps would not have agreed to study a particular song or attempted an awkward vocal passage without the encouragement and goading of friends within the group. It is perhaps encouraging for a singer to see someone else in the group achieve something, in that it spurs them on to have a go too. This certainly can apply to sight-singing studies, technical exercises or improvisation, where a more reluctant student can be encouraged to try again by their friends. A small element of challenge and even competition can help with group study. Each member should take on responsibility for the success of the group study.   HP
>
> An element of healthy competition can be very useful, though this clearly needs some sensitivity. Target setting (and recording) is perhaps not as easy as it is with individual lessons, but – with the exception of very young beginners – there is no reason why pupils should not make notes of what to practise themselves, if the teacher reserves some time at the end of the lesson to make the options clear.   MR

Rewards

Challenges that are met should be acknowledged and celebrated. Of course it is vital that pupils' successes are praised and encouraged and that enjoyment of music-making should be a reward in itself. Many of the teacher-contributors also point out the value of rather more tangible ways of marking progress. For younger pupils, especially, and for those in the early stages of playing, such rewards can be particularly motivating and inspiring.

I find giving suggested practice targets useful: for beginners this would be four times a week for 10–15 minutes. 'Rewards' for reaching the target seem to motivate most younger children. These could be a sticker for four practices and a bigger reward once six stickers have been achieved. Comparing practice diaries is something that seems to arise from this. While it can be useful and motivational, there has to be caution as some children have more parental input and support than others. Targets must be achievable but not too easy either. Setting individual targets is important, as some pupils will not be able to manage what others can. The teacher has to be flexible to individual needs; this can be hard in the group situation. Most pupils manage to achieve their bigger reward once a term.

Certificates are also useful especially for younger students. Small achievements need to be recognized for beginner string players, as the difficulties and challenges of the instruments are so great. A 'Super practiser' award or a 'Wonderful bow-hold' certificate, which can be home-made on the computer, can help motivate. If the school has a house points system, giving points can both raise the profile of instrumental lessons and motivate good practice routines.   KB

Although the same motivational techniques can be employed with pupils learning in groups as for those who have individual lessons, in a group context the pupils themselves may respond differently to the strategies you use. A good example of this is giving out gold stars or other merit awards. When I give a gold star to a pupil who I teach individually, the pupil will compare their performance this week with that over previous weeks where they have or have not received stars. From this they will gauge whether or not I am particularly pleased with their progress on this occasion. In a group situation, however, rather than understanding the receipt of the star in the context of their personal development, pupils tend to compare themselves with others in the group, noting which pupils did and did not receive stars this week. This illustrates the essential competitiveness and comparison that is a normal part of a child's development, self-awareness and learning. While rewards can be a wonderful way of encouraging children when they make good progress, it is important for teachers to be sensitive to the child's emotional development.   AE

Matching work to pupils' ability

Perhaps the most effective way of promoting and supporting good progress is for teachers to ensure that the work provided in lessons and beyond is carefully matched to pupils' abilities; in other words, that it is not too easy, that it is challenging, yet not over-demanding. In group teaching, where pupils often learn at different rates and can soon be at varying stages of ability within the same group, there are particular challenges for the teacher.

I try to encompass everyone's musical abilities with exercises that all can participate in. For example:

1   Sing a simple phrase and ask the pupils to sing it back. Then ask them to describe the note values or pitches. This could be by using conventional notation or their own notation (long note, short note, phrase goes up or down, and so on).

2   Look at the music on the page. Ask the pupils to spot rhythmic patterns or melodic sequences. See if they can clap or tap a rhythmic pattern in the music. Ask them to tap the pulse and sing the rhythm.

3   Using flash cards, ask the group to clap the rhythms. See if they can remember a sequence of rhythms after looking at them for a few seconds.

4   Within the group, sing a tonic triad. Then form other chords by having one person change their note while the others hold their original notes. Discuss how the chord has changed.

5   Sing a scale using the numbers one to eight. Next, replace one of the numbers with a different sound – a clap or a finger click, for example. Change the number that is replaced or have more than one number replaced at the same time. Each number that is replaced could have a different sound. Ask the pupils to invent some body percussion for the sounds. Remember to sing up and down the scale. This can be great fun and often catches someone out!

6   Divide the group in two and ask one half to start singing a scale from the top and the other from the bottom. Listen to the harmonies that are formed. Add a rhythmic challenge by marching on the spot at the same time. Change the time signature to give the scale a different feel.

7   Sing a scale up and down. Then switch between silent singing and normal singing, according to an agreed gesture from a group member. Speed up the frequency of the switch, and see who you can catch out! Group members could take turns at directing.

8   It is always best to teach songs voice to voice, particularly if a member of the group has problems with pitch. Make sure that all the singers are secure with the song. It is very easy for a weaker voice to hide behind a strong voice, which means they never really learn the song properly. Split the group up and get members to sing difficult passages individually or in pairs.   HP

Often it is not helpful for pupils to be provided with exactly the same material and for them to be expected to find their own level. They need to be provided with different challenges within the same group task. Differentiation – understanding the various levels of ability within the group and providing activities and materials to suit these –

is the cornerstone of successful group teaching. Successful differentiation can be achieved with good planning and careful consideration of how each component of a group task can be suitably matched to each pupil.

Coping with differentiation is perhaps easier with percussion, given a complete range of instruments. We can simply give instruments or voices to individuals according to musical ability. I include here clapping or body percussion as an instrument. The important management skill for the teacher is *scoring* the group lesson. Simple instruments and simple instrumental lines can be scored to play a very important part.   PC

Once different ability levels and rates of progress become apparent, carefully choose ensemble music which allows for this without the pupils knowing. Ensure the weakest is given a part or activity they can succeed at in ensemble playing, even though they may attempt more challenging tasks individually.   RW/RC

I find that the fastest learner in the group usually has a positive effect on the others, inspiring them to make quicker progress. It is less usual for the slower learner to have an adverse effect on the others. Sometimes, however, the slower learner will be discouraged, so it is important to provide differentiated material to enable all the pupils to learn at their own pace.   AE

There are always different abilities within any given group, and this is the most challenging aspect of group teaching. Even the most able student will not necessarily be strong in every area, so the teacher has to recognize and exploit the strengths and weaknesses of each student. For example, a fluent reader may be in the same group as someone who finds reading music more of a challenge. One approach could be to develop playing by ear or rote to allow both students to work together. The most able need not be moved on to the next stage: it can be just as productive to go sideways with a piece and perhaps give the able student some extension activity. Adding things like dynamics, slurs or rhythmic variations can provide interest for the more able student, while still keeping the group working together. Providing supplementary material for students to work on at home can keep interest going; it is important that the able don't get bored and that the less able do not feel left behind.

For less able students, use any props that might help – write in fingering, letter names or whatever may be useful. Using a highlighter pen at the beginning and the end of a line can help those with reading difficulties. This is especially useful when doing duets or trios, as it helps keep the eye on the correct line. Differentiated material has to be used at times – usually written by the teacher. Making up simple ostinato parts that can be taught by rote can keep everyone involved: some play this while others play a more complex line.

> At times students need to be regrouped so that they are working alongside students who are progressing at a similar pace. **KB**

From time to time, some group teachers will therefore feel it useful to regroup their pupils to accommodate widening diversity of ability levels.

> The first strategy has to be to encourage as many pupils as possible to commit themselves to learning an instrument. With several groups learning, the problem of matching students into appropriate levels becomes quite straightforward. **RPe**
>
> Where differentiation becomes more marked, I would usually try to reorganize groups to provide a better match within each group in a school. The popularity of electronic keyboard makes this possible in most instances, but I realize that where instruments are less well subscribed, group reorganization is often not an option, and individual tuition is consequently more likely to be required. **AE**

Monitoring progress

Providing differentiated tasks for pupils in groups goes some way to ensuring that they make satisfactory and better progress because the focus of the teaching is on individual achievement within a group context. However, such progress needs to be monitored regularly, though this is not onerous if it is seen as a component of the teaching cycle. Monitoring is part of the regular, formative assessment process which results from effective planning, from knowing what pupils should be taught and from recognizing how they have responded, what they have learnt and what the next step will be for them individually or as a group.

Different types of assessment

p. 118 →

Different levels of planning

p. 111 →

Planning for the short term, in the form of weekly lesson plans, however brief, provides an opportunity for the teacher not only to set out what is intended to be covered in the weekly lesson but also to record what the pupils achieved – the outcomes.

> Lesson plans and notes are used for each group to record aims and outcomes, etc. This monitoring is prescribed but has to be fairly flexible – lesson plans have to be fluid enough to adapt to questions arising during a lesson. **KB**
>
> Keep a brief record of activities and objectives. Look at where the pupils are and where they might be by the end of the session. Be realistic about what can be achieved in that time and be prepared for development and change. A group may

respond differently from how you expected; the intuitive teacher will move the goalposts and change the plan for the next lesson. It is useful to keep a note of the repertoire being studied, effective exercises and games (what worked and what didn't), the vocal history of the pupil, information on other instruments they are learning, grades achieved, weak areas, strong areas, and so on. Encourage the pupils within the group to keep a diary of things to be practised and studied throughout the week. They might also like to write down how the practice went and report back any difficulties or triumphs in the next lesson. HP

Group targets are useful as well as individual ones. Use a grid with separate categories and tick-boxes, showing what pupils have achieved in different areas. Depending on the age of the pupil, this could be discussed with them in advance. As this kind of formative assessment is an important part of the teaching and learning process, teachers shouldn't feel apologetic about using class time to do it.

It is important to bear in mind that monitoring the progress of individuals is very important to them, whereas monitoring the progress of the class as a whole is a very important aspect of being a 'reflective practitioner'. In either case, monitoring progress is not really possible without long-term objectives. Perhaps even more importantly than in individual lessons, short-, mid- and long-term planning needs to be effective and efficient. Teachers need to think as much about skill acquisition and knowledge building as about the pieces and exercises that get pupils to that point. MR

...may respond differently from how you expected...

Assessment is not a one-way process. It can be at its most effective when the pupils are involved in making a judgement about how they are doing and what they need to do to improve. Target setting is a useful tool for establishing criteria by which progress is to be assessed.

When assessing, recording and reporting on large numbers of pupils in a group situation, it is helpful to learn from our classroom colleagues. The teacher should have a clear idea of where the group as a whole should have got to over a period of time. This medium-term planning and target setting should be discussed and agreed with the pupils as part of the lesson process. Usually some of this will be put into the practice diary so that they can understand where the week-to-week practice goals fit into the longer-term strategy. It is then much easier to adopt an 'exception marking' scheme, where one has to note only when a pupil is clearly doing better or worse than expected. There will be clear points during the term where discussion can take place and the pupils will be aware of how they are doing because of the target-setting process. If parents take the time to read the practice diary, they too will be better informed as to what is going on and will understand where the teacher and pupils are going. Examinations come into the overall strategy but, until recent developments, they were a poor indicator of how a player would perform in an ensemble situation. This could lead to misunderstanding between parents and teachers as to the placing of players in ensembles. I hope the development of the Music Medals scheme will start to improve this.   RPr

16

Music Medals

Group teaching, then, can provide an effective vehicle for assessing both the individual and the whole group.

12

Assessment for groups

I have a curriculum of work and a guide to how long it should take to complete. Progress can be mapped against this plan. I ensure that pupils are always completely informed and aware of where their work fits into the curriculum. Progress is presented as criteria-based outcomes, and as easily recognizable increments. A path through the curriculum is offered, suggested and encouraged, but pupils are also empowered to take control of their individual progress path.

It is the very nature of group teaching that offers the element of change, variation and improvisation required to maintain energy in a curriculum.

Success for an individual within a group setting can very often be simply that their playing is successful within a group. Playing a pop groove at the drum kit in a one-to-one setting will offer the possibility for a technical appraisal, but that individual does not yet know if this can work as it is designed to. A pop groove must drive a band and energize bass, guitar and others. It must be there to make the singer sound good and encourage an audience to get up and dance. It must also provide the function of bar and phrase geography, and be a time framework for the band. In a one-to-one situation, pupil and teacher will not hear if these things are present. Monitoring progress and enabling assessment require that this pop groove is taken into the group setting; then we can know that it works and is therefore a successful outcome.

A group setting for me is where real music-making can happen. If the group is making music then we have success. The very act of group activity, therefore, supplies a very natural assessment procedure. PC

The assessment process is integral to teaching and learning, but it should not drive the instrumental curriculum. Summative assessment, such as graded examinations, provides staging posts in pupils' musical progress for them to celebrate their achievements and to motivate and aid their musical development. However, it is worth remembering that much of our assessment of pupils is formative and diagnostic, and comes from weekly observation and discussion with our pupils. Only some of this assessment is recorded or reported to parents. The following adage rings true for instrumental teaching: 'We assess more than we record; we record more than we report.'

13

Feedback and reporting

In conclusion

Group teaching can enable pupils to succeed and to make progress, individually and together. Good group-teaching occurs when the group is well motivated, when pupils are sufficiently challenged and rewarded, when the individual's ability is successfully catered for within the group and when progress is monitored sufficiently to enable each one to improve and to achieve as well as he or she is able.

I try to encourage progress by:

- inspiring the pupils to love music and want to play well;
- giving pupils a broad overview of the work being done over the next term or two;
- setting clear expectations (to both the group and to individuals within the group) from one week to the next;
- recognizing achievement by awarding regular 'gold stars' and more occasional 'excellence awards';
- organizing opportunities for pupils to perform as often as feasible;
- exposing pupils to more advanced players (in concerts, for example);
- using more advanced students as assistant teachers – this particularly inspires the younger players, as well as giving the more advanced players an opportunity to develop teaching and communication skills. AE

7

Using music technology

Brian Ley

There can be little doubt that, in the last few years, information technology (IT) has been a major influence in all our lives. There is hardly any area of life that is not now pervaded by technology, and in education the study of information and communication technology (ICT) is a core experience for pupils through virtually every subject on the curriculum. The music industry and music education have been strongly influenced by ICT, or 'music technology' as it is more commonly known.

During classroom music lessons, in the primary and especially the secondary sector, it is quite common for pupils to work with a variety of music technology, from audio playback and recording facilities to computers and software. These are designed to broaden pupils' musical experience and develop their musical understanding and learning. In the past music technology was used less in instrumental teaching, though more and more instrumental teachers now recognize that it has opened up many new opportunities to support and enhance musical learning for their pupils. Moreover, many find that pupils are already fully conversant with many aspects of music technology (to which they often have access at home) and that it is a strong motivating force in their musical study. A number of teachers are also realizing that music technology is a powerful teaching tool as well as a sophisticated learning resource. The purpose of this chapter is to outline the types of music technology that can be used in instrumental lessons.

Music technology can be very useful in group teaching. However, care should be taken when determining how and when it is used. Visiting instrumental teachers may need to be aware of a school's own technology policy before using computers in lessons. If the use of such technology involves pupils searching the Internet, either in school or at home, then teachers should be conversant with issues of child protection as well as

...already fully conversant with many aspects of music technology...

the laws governing copyright, if material is being downloaded. Teachers should also be aware that music technology is simply another resource and needs to be used selectively. Like any resource, it needs to be relevant to the learning needs of pupils. It is not worth using in instrumental lessons, or for homework, if it does not aid the pupils' musical learning.

The National Curriculum and ICT

ICT is required to be delivered through all National Curriculum subjects. The curriculum sets out, more specifically, the progression in musical learning through the three key stages:

Key Stage 1 (5–7 years)

Pupils could use software designed to enable exploration of sounds. They could use recording equipment to recall sounds and identify and make improvements.

(The use of ICT is a non-statutory requirement at Key Stage 1, although teachers are encouraged to teach it where appropriate.)

Key Stage 2 (7–11 years)

Pupils should be taught the knowledge, skills and understanding through using ICT to capture, change and combine sounds.

Key Stage 3 (11–14 years)

Pupils should be taught the knowledge, skills and understanding through using ICT to create, manipulate and refine sounds.

(National Curriculum 2000)

There are just a few other specific references to ICT in the Programmes of Study at Key Stages 2 and 3:

Key Stage 2

4c. Pupils should be taught how music is produced in different ways (for example, through the use of different resources, including ICT) and described through relevant established and invented notations.

Key Stage 3

4c. Pupils should be taught to identify the resources, conventions, processes and procedures, including the use of ICT, staff notation and other relevant notations, used in selected musical genres, styles and traditions.

4d. Pupils should be taught to identify the contextual influences that affect the way music is created, performed and heard (for example, the impact of ICT).

(National Curriculum 2000)

At Key Stage 4 (GCSE examination), and in AS- and A-level courses, pupils can take options in music technology. It is generally expected that pupils will use music technology at some stage in these courses.

From the 1990s, instrumental teaching gradually became more closely aligned to the rationale and content of the National Curriculum. This approach to instrumental teaching is now codified in publications such as *A Common Approach 2002*. These provide a framework for an instrumental and vocal curriculum that identifies areas of musical experience (skills in listening and performing, improvising and composing, and appraising) which are common to those which pupils encounter in the music classroom. Additionally, there is a desire on the part of the government and others in education that many more pupils should be given the opportunity to learn to play a musical instrument and to engage in music-making at all levels and of all types and genres. This desire for a more inclusive instrumental curriculum challenges many instrumental teachers, especially those working for LEA Music Services, to expand their thinking and ways of working. For example, some visiting instrumental teachers may be required at some point during the week to cope with whole classes or with larger groups – of up to, say, ten pupils – and with mixed ensembles. For some, adopting new approaches to teaching can be daunting enough without the need to take on board music technology too. Yet music technology provides alternative ways to support teaching and learning, without compromising musical integrity. The rest of this chapter looks at music technology in the context of instrumental teaching, examines the rationale for its use and explores various ways in which teachers are currently using it in their own teaching.

What is music technology?

Music technology may be defined as any electronic device (hardware or software) that enables the user to access, control, manipulate or communicate musical information. This may include:

- audio and video playback and recording;
- electronic keyboards;
- sound processors;
- computers, using associated software and the Internet.

For many years, it has been common for teachers to use audio playback and recording facilities in their teaching, to enable their pupils to listen to and compare performances of pieces they are studying, or to record work in progress so that it can be evaluated or assessed. More recently, however, teachers have begun to recognize the potential of other forms of music technology, finding alternative ways of supporting and enhancing their pupils' musical learning.

Why use music technology?

Being motivated and having fun with music technology does not necessarily mean that effective learning is taking place, so we need to be sure about why we use it in instrumental lessons.

> I use keyboards in schools when there is no piano available. Many pupils have these at home and can play scales to a rhythm backing to add variety to scale practice. I also use CD backings in my group teaching. If a whole group is playing along to a backing track, the teacher can be freed up to point to the music for younger readers or provide support in other ways. I have found that students are more motivated to practise if they have a recording or CD backing to use at home. For older pupils, extending their listening by lending them CDs is useful for introducing them to new repertoire and artists: this can lead to interesting discussions during a group lesson once the whole group has listened to a particular CD. I use Sibelius (music notation setting and playback software) for writing and arranging music; this is often bespoke arrangements for particular groups. **KB**

Music technology can make teaching and learning easier. For example, notation software programs allow the teacher to provide, easily and quickly, tailor-made arrangements for mixed-ability groups.

For many pupils, especially those who may falter with aspects of technique or who may struggle in a group lesson, the technology can take away the mystique of music and reveal its magic. Music technology can provide a sophistication and immediacy of sound that can 'lift' pupils' playing. Because it can be easy for pupils to use, it increases their interaction with the music itself and supports the development of playing, performing and creative skills.

Music technology in practice

Music technology allows pupils to develop practical skills and musical understanding through three areas of musical learning, which were originally identified through research carried out in the Music and ICT Project undertaken by the British Educational Communications and Technology Agency (Becta) from 1997 to 2001. These three areas of learning relate easily to instrumental teaching and learning, and are discussed below.

Using and investigating sounds and structures

Music technology enables teachers and pupils alike to develop their creativity in ways that can further support musical learning and the development of instrumental skills. These include creating and recording sound, using notation and sequencing packages to create compositions and arrangements, and creating performance materials.

> Music technology provides the capacity to bypass notation, if pupils have creative ideas which exceed their notational skill (with luck, this is fairly common), or indeed to acquire notational skills by making a link between sound and symbol, if not in the conventional way. It enables compositions to build up gradually – sifting and replacing, etc.
>
> MR
>
> Score-writing software allows you to produce tidy, legible parts for ensemble playing.
>
> RW/RC

As noted above, teachers can indeed provide their own arrangements of pieces specially tailored for the group's needs. Score-writing software can also be used effectively to introduce pupils to notation by their exploring and placing notes on a screen, which are then played back through the computer's soundcard. Elementary improvisations can also be set up, where the teacher provides a template score with a few notes missing: the pupil plays the written score and fills in the gaps with improvised sounds. At a more advanced level, notation programs can be used to provide a full score of a piece, where any or all of the parts can be muted on playback to enable pupils to play a solo line against a backing track.

Alternatively, sequencing software allows direct access to sound, which can be easily recorded (from an electronic keyboard, for instance) and then copied, pasted and layered into a musical structure. Many teachers use such software to create backing tracks for pupils to play along with (see below).

Recording pupils' work, on tape, mini-disc or computer, is another effective use of music technology. The pupils could be fully involved in the recording process and afterwards evaluate their own and others' contributions. In recording performances, some thought needs to be given to how much rehearsal and what sort of preparation are needed, and to how the sense and spirit of the music are to be communicated. In a group situation this means developing ensemble skills so that the performance is as good as it can be. In addition, issues such as the placing of the microphone to achieve balance between individual parts help develop pupils' listening skills and their musical understanding.

Another area where pupils may use and investigate sounds and structures is through the use of multimedia CD-ROMs, where they can develop musical ideas for instrumental homework. There are many CD-ROMs on the market, of various types. They range from those which focus on different styles and conventions in music (on Baroque music, for example, or the life and work of a particular composer) to those that are more creative and allow some interaction between the user and the computer; the latter might include instrumental tutors or programs which allow some editing of musical material. CD-ROMs are quite straightforward to use, and can encourage active learning. However, teachers should ensure that such multimedia resources are suitable for their pupils and that they really focus on music and musical learning rather than just providing peripheral information.

The Internet can also be an outstanding creative musical resource for both teachers and pupils. In addition to sites specifically related to music education, which are often in the form of teacher notes and plans, there are thousands of sites that provide music for teachers and pupils to interact with – to explore, research, manipulate, rearrange or use as the basis for improvisation and composition. The Internet allows instrumental teachers to have access to relevant materials that are flexible enough to be adapted to both the requirements of their particular curriculum and to reflect the needs of pupils. Again, teachers need to evaluate and use this material before recommending particular sites to pupils.

There are many specific ways in which Internet resources can enrich the music curriculum. The Internet can:

- provide a wealth of audio and MIDI examples, for listening and as the basis for practical musical activity;
- encourage the development of performing, improvising and composing skills;
- extend musical knowledge and understanding;

- enable the exchange of musical ideas and compositions with others worldwide (via e-mail), and thereby
- stimulate performance and composition;
- enable and encourage pupils to listen to a wide variety of music.

However, this rich resource can equally be a source of frustration, irrelevance and inappropriateness, unless sites are specifically related to the needs of teachers and their pupils. Access needs to be quick and reliable and sites need to be relevant, informative and firmly linked to the objectives of the instrumental curriculum and to clear learning expectations. Care should also be taken to ensure that, when downloading music and music-related materials, copyright is respected. Note too that some material can be accessed and downloaded only at a cost.

For instrumental teachers who work in schools, it is worth remembering that the school itself will probably have a policy on the use of computers and associated technology. This might include a code of practice on how and when pupils use the Internet, and visiting teachers need to be aware of any such policy. It is rarely feasible for instrumental teachers to have live access to the Internet in the school teaching room. Nevertheless, teacher resource material can still be downloaded for use offline, and pupils can access material on the Internet from home. If you ask your pupils to do this, make sure they understand that they need to get permission from their parents before using the Internet for this purpose.

Refining and enhancing performance

Music technology can be used effectively to help pupils to improve their overall performance. Perhaps the most widely used technological resource here is the backing track, where a CD, tape, computer program or electronic keyboard is used to supply a musical backing, to which pupils listen and over which they practise, play and perform. (Even non-keyboard players will find it relatively simple to set up and use backing tracks on a keyboard.) Because backing tracks are frequently of high quality, they often motivate and stimulate pupils to perform to their best. They can also be used as a backing for sight-reading exercises, for improvisations and for providing a harmonic background for, say, a twelve-bar blues.

8

Improvising and composing

The use of electronic keyboard auto-accompaniments and the full resources available on digital keyboards is a fundamental part of my own musical involvement with my pupils, and of the skills that I teach them.

I make use of basic playback, and I make interactive use of MIDI files within the electronic keyboards themselves, utilizing the floppy disk drive as a playback and editing interface for sequenced material prepared by me before the lesson. With more able students, I also use the record facility within the lesson. I also use a laptop computer as an integral part of my teaching – including Sibelius 2 software for score creation; Cubasis VST, Cubase SX, Reason, and Ableton Live for music production; and Dance eJay 5 for entry-level music technology at primary school level (lunchtime club).   AE

My main use of ICT is to give players an accompaniment or a model to use at home. This can use MIDI accompaniments or recordings I have made for them. With MIDI accompaniments I can give students their pieces played at a variety of tempi to allow them to build step by step. This can be done easily and cheaply with floppy disks. I also provide accompaniments for scale work. With my laptop, I can control which parts are played and the balance.   RPe

For some instrumental disciplines, such as percussion or steel pans, the use of backing tracks has become an essential part of the teaching process. For others backing tracks are an invaluable support to teaching.

I use music technology all the time. Using audio playback, drum machines, sequencing software or hardware provides a backing track to the lesson or lesson segment. Music can be in the room as pupils step into the learning space. Simple use of a volume control can then allow some simple spoken instructions to pupils, creating some activity that joins the backing track. It is important that pupils understand that the backing track runs continuously through this learning segment. Activity number one can pause, with the volume reduced, then more spoken instructions given to take pupils to the next incremental step. The volume is then turned back up and another joining-in and 'doing' activity begins. Pupils are involved in learning, but importantly they leave the room with a backing track to that learning in their head. They will recall the backing track much as they remember tunes they hear on the radio. With this recall and memory will come the learning opportunity that they experienced.

My approach to using ICT in a group or with individuals is similar. The added benefit of using the backing-track technique in a group is that it helps group discipline because the backing track is always there. Whatever happens within the group musically, or whatever happens to the discipline within the group, the participants will be doing something along with the backing track. Therefore, we have *some* learning going on.   PC

In both individual and group teaching I use drum machines. A drum machine may assist the percussion section – and in some cases it is the only form of percussion. TC

It is also possible to obtain MIDI files from the Internet. The Internet has a wealth of songs which can be downloaded to form a backing track.   HP

75

Many teachers use recordings of pupils' work as the basis for their own assessment and for the pupils themselves to evaluate and to improve their own performances. Recordings enable performances to be stored and reviewed as work in progress; in the group pupils can discuss each other's performances and learn from them. A recording of finished work, perhaps together with other previous recordings, can fairly easily be burned to an audio CD on a computer so that pupils have a record of work over a period of time.

Video recording can be a very supportive tool, not just for singers – as outlined below – but for any instrumental teacher.

Child
protection

p. 134 →

For those people lucky enough to have access to a video camera, film a performance of your pupils and watch it together. It is most revealing when singers can stand back from a performance and watch themselves in action (rather than watching in a mirror, though that is also valuable). The students can see exactly what they are doing and are often surprised by the results.

It is also beneficial to keep a record of the group or individual pupils' work on tape or video. Pupils can then start to see the improvements that they have made over a long period of time.   HP

Some teachers also find that using video to record their own teaching is invaluable in helping them to monitor and evaluate their own style and its impact on their pupils. If teachers are using a video to record pupils' work, in any form, then the necessary permission must be sought from the school and from the parents.

Extending knowledge of music history, music theory and musical styles

In earlier chapters we have been reminded of the importance of listening as a fundamental experience of music and music-making. Music technology can provide opportunities for pupils to develop and refine their listening skills. Pupils can listen to recordings of pieces they are learning, or to similar pieces for the purpose of comparison, either by means of standard audio playback (CD or tape, for example) or by accessing music in various forms on the Internet. Pupils could use CD-ROMs to learn about music and the background of composers and other performers; this could provide a stimulus for their own music-making. It is also possible for pupils and teachers to exchange musical ideas, materials and information via the Internet and e-mail.

Listening

← p. 36

Computer technology can also effectively support aural training and the development of musical knowledge.

Computer software can be used for aural development (Auralia, Hearmaster etc.), particularly where these allow for a continuous record of assessment of skills mastered, and allow students to develop their aural skills in private.   MR

When to use music technology

It is neither practical nor desirable to include every one of the above examples in instrumental lessons. Nor should music technology necessarily form a part of every lesson – teachers should use the technology appropriately in order to aid pupils' learning. In its research the Music and ICT Project described the three stages when music technology can contribute to and integrate with other music activities: before, alongside and after. Here are some examples for instrumental teaching of how the technology could be used by the teacher, the pupil, or both working together.

Before other musical activities:

- introducing new musical ideas;
- presenting performance models;
- providing raw information to act upon;
- helping to reinforce knowledge before moving on.

Alongside other musical activities:

- providing flexible accompaniments for instrumental performance;
- providing for differentiated tasks;
- recording work in progress.

After other musical activities:

- providing further support;
- recording and storing work in progress;
- recording completed work for presentation;
- offering related examples for comparison;
- enabling communication worldwide.

In conclusion

Whether working in groups or one-to-one, music technology can be a powerful medium for learning. Used properly, it can be a very effective teaching and learning resource. However, as outlined in Becta's *Music Technology in Action* training booklet, there are some important principles to consider:

- Music technology should serve the cause of instrumental teaching and learning, not dictate its direction.
- Music technology should not exclude other current and traditional teaching approaches – it complements rather than replaces other musical activities.
- Many pupils have a greater technical expertise in using music technology than their teachers; such expertise should be welcomed and exploited.
- Whether it be in using traditional instruments or in using music technology, the teacher's role is to facilitate and enable the most effective learning from pupils.

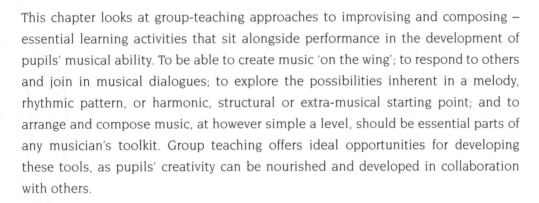

8

Improvising and composing for groups

Joanna Glover and Nigel Scaife

This chapter looks at group-teaching approaches to improvising and composing – essential learning activities that sit alongside performance in the development of pupils' musical ability. To be able to create music 'on the wing'; to respond to others and join in musical dialogues; to explore the possibilities inherent in a melody, rhythmic pattern, or harmonic, structural or extra-musical starting point; and to arrange and compose music, at however simple a level, should be essential parts of any musician's toolkit. Group teaching offers ideal opportunities for developing these tools, as pupils' creativity can be nourished and developed in collaboration with others.

Historically, instrumental training was far more aurally based and creative than tends to be the case today. Before the end of the eighteenth century most professional musicians could improvise, and little distinction was made between the all-round practising musician and the specialist composer. But from the twentieth century, the main educational focus for musical creativity has been on the creation of musical 'products' rather than on self-expression through spontaneously created music, even though improvisation remains an important feature of much popular and traditional music around the world. (One of the reasons for this is that improvisation has too often been regarded as a pre-compositional activity, rather than a form of music-making in its own right.) Yet improvising, arranging and composing can each make a significant contribution to the musical development of group-taught students; these activities also help significantly to draw instrumental learning into a musical context that more closely parallels classroom music experiences.

Teachers who embrace improvisation and composition in group lessons harness a propulsive musical energy that supports all other aspects of instrumental or vocal teaching and learning. While to some it may feel daunting at first, creative work rapidly becomes second nature to teacher and pupils alike. When lesson time is limited, finding opportunities for these activities might seem difficult – yet with the strategies below, teachers can quickly and effectively develop their pupils' creativity. In turn, this creativity can accelerate and enhance the acquisition of technical, interpretative and expressive skills.

Developing creativity

Some instrumental teachers may feel that creative work is low on their list of priorities, outside their remit or simply too difficult. But in fact introducing creativity into group lessons makes room for, and builds on, natural musical behaviour. Young children are naturally creative with sound. They make music as part of their repertoire of 'play', which is, by definition, endlessly improvisational. In the early years they move easily between speech and song and play freely with sound, creating their own musical patterns for pure enjoyment. They borrow snatches of songs they hear and incorporate them into their own music. Some of their songs are recreated again and again, often with new developments and interpretations. None of these activities is dependent on adult encouragement or teaching – they are an intrinsic part of children's development. If approached in this way, pupils' early confidence and musicianship can be developed and sustained. If pupils are to develop as all-round musicians, it is essential that their creativity is harnessed – that they should not only play music but also play *with* music.

Play is vital to creative development. Most learners tackling a new musical instrument are drawn at some stage into doodling out of curiosity or for fun – often as an 'off-task' activity when they are supposed to be practising scales and pieces. Playing imaginary music, or pretending to play music not yet learnt, are other components of practice time. Experimenting with new notes, techniques or ideas is also common behaviour that should be encouraged and valued. The group situation offers scope for collaborative 'play' which allows pupils to interact musically in a situation that is informal and fun – and which may be more mutually supportive and less intimidating than the one-to-one environment. 'Playing' musically in groups often frees pupils to play more expressively and dramatically than they might alone; it also aids awareness of ensemble interaction. Teaching that does not capitalize on play as well as playing misses key opportunities for developing aural and technical skill; musical awareness, sensitivity and imagination; and, above all, the player's sense of his or her own musical voice. Teachers who concentrate solely on the performance of pieces and the acquisition of technique deprive their pupils of a rich vein of musical experience.

The teacher's role

In this context the teacher's role is to make opportunities, listen wisely, and encourage students to feel confident in their musical responses and inventiveness. Most pupils have plenty of their own ideas and will be motivated to offer these through improvising, composing and arranging once they realize that a teacher listens to and values what they bring. If teachers trust and work with students' ideas, however simply at first, the results can be transforming. And because they start to gain insight into how music is created, into its potential as a medium, pupils begin to listen harder, think more about everything they play, and respect and try out each other's ideas. Teachers can draw out and build on what is offered by individual students and find ways to use this within the group.

Teachers should also offer a rich, stimulating programme by introducing new musical ideas and techniques, enabling students to try these in different ways. Widening awareness of musical elements, choices, devices and styles enriches pupils' musical imagination. Much of this awareness may be drawn from repertoire being learnt, from listening to recorded music and from teacher demonstration. The use of music technology further motivates: it enables students to capture, listen to, create, mix and edit music and gives them a sense of ownership and of connection to the wider musical world. Realistically, given limitations of time and resources, teachers have to maintain a balance in the teaching programme by integrating these aspects into group activities and by encouraging and capitalizing on what students can achieve between lessons.

7

Using music technology

Playing by ear

Improvising and composing worry some teachers. They may feel daunted by leaving the written page behind and creating music in the moment or inventing it from scratch. Reassurance comes only from listening to what pupils produce and so is not available in advance. 'Running on faith' and being willing to take risks are therefore crucial to the quality of the results. If such work is new to the teacher – it is unlikely to be new to children – it is best to take small steps towards letting go of performing exclusively from notation. Asking pupils to play well-known tunes by ear is a good place to start moving away from printed music.

Playing by ear helps pupils to develop the ear-to-hand co-ordination skills to play what they hear in their 'mind's ear'. It integrates mind and body, aiding that vital process of internalization – 'thinking in sound'. Many pupils who are encouraged to play by ear early on become better sight-readers later, as they more easily make the connection between symbol and sound. Playing by ear, as playing from memory, helps pupils to make 'mind-maps' of a piece, internalizing contours, landmarks and cues and being free to focus on expressive features.

Once pupils can play a tune by ear, ask them to play just the first section and make up their own continuation. This activity can be shared around the group, with the 'known' section alternating with new phrases. Well-known tunes can be used to introduce rhythmic or melodic decoration, making embellishment fun. More advanced pupils might be asked to play well-known tunes in different keys.

> So much of the technical content of the lesson can be covered without music that it actually makes the whole process much easier. No music stands, reading difficulties and difficult passages to get in the way – problems are isolated. This does involve the teacher in moving around, being energetic and watching all of the pupils all of the time.
>
> RW/RC

Why improvise?

Improvising enables pupils to explore musical patterns and processes, to develop their musical imagination and to learn by listening and playing together. The immediate feedback of making and hearing establishes musical cause and effect: 'If I do this, it sounds like that.' This development of musical self-awareness facilitates the progress of instrumental technique, musical invention, and understanding of how the elements of music interact. It also parallels the way we learn other skills and concepts – through curiosity, playful experimentation and sensory feedback. Ultimately, improvisation goes further, since it generates music that is of aesthetic value in itself.

Using improvisation from the earliest stages of learning has many benefits for teachers and pupils in a group context. It develops:

- group musical interaction, communication and sense of ensemble;
- the connection between pupil and instrument, allowing the pupil to 'speak' more directly through the instrument and find a musical 'voice';
- skills of listening and responding and the collaborative process of creating and interpreting music;
- musical contexts in which to address technical issues, such as a new articulation style or finger pattern.

In a teaching approach that regularly incorporates improvisation, each new step, whether in note-learning, scales, dynamic devices, and so on, can be developed and consolidated. The technical and expressive aspects of playing can be brought together, each driving the other. New technical skills reveal new expressive possibilities, while seeking expression motivates learners to improve their technique. Improvisation may also be used to develop aural skills and generate ideas for composition. It also facilitates group communication, including teacher–pupil interaction, as improvising in a group encourages teachers to face pupils, not be next to or behind them as when reading from notation, and it encourages pupils to use eye contact when playing.

> Improvisation is a regular feature of all my group teaching. I regard it as a crucial skill which should be developed in a structured way. I also find that pupils not only enjoy improvisation but generally find it easier and more approachable than many other (more traditional) aspects of learning to play. When improvising, pupils often play music that is both more technically advanced than what they meet playing written music, and more complex in its language. For example, pupils might effectively improvise in compound time before they have been introduced to compound time-signatures or fully understood the concept of dividing the beat into three subdivisions. Improvisation is therefore not only worthwhile in its own right but it is a useful vehicle for introducing other technical and musical aspects of playing. In my own teaching, improvisation will certainly be introduced in the first term's lessons, and often in the very first lesson. AE

Early creative processes

As activities in instrumental lessons provide opportunities for pupils to improvise, compose and arrange their own music, the processes through which they do so begin to emerge. Through listening and discussion, teachers can begin to hear and understand something of how pupils' musical imaginations are working. This is invaluable in developing aural and interpretative skills. Below are some of the most common early processes for creating music. Of course, individuals work in different ways, so this must be viewed as an observational guide and certainly not as a set of exclusive categories.

Action led

Early improvisation and composition on an instrument is, for obvious reasons, greatly influenced by the feeling of the fingers or patterns of other bodily movements already learnt. Because so much early instrumental work is based on repetition, early creative attempts tend to be 'made as played' – that is, dominated by techniques inherent in the playing of the instrument, involving fingering, breathing, and so on. Consequently, early inventions may not sound all that inventive. They may also be more felt than heard, an interesting feature of much early instrumental work. Young children and beginners often pattern actions rather than sounds. There are, however, plenty of musicians and composers who have worked in exactly this way, and it can be a rich and intriguing source of ideas.

Concept led

Some pupils find it easier to invent music if they have a conceptual framework for it. This may be a number pattern, such as 'three on every note'; a musical shape, 'up then down again'; or an idea of using symmetry or opposites. With some instruments this may tie up with visual concepts or patterns, such as 'all the black keys' on a keyboard, or 'from smallest to largest' on a drum kit.

Drama led

Here the player invents music according to an unfolding drama (either pre-planned or evolved 'on the wing'). Children sometimes accompany improvisation with narrative, or vice versa, and the music is led by events and moods required by character or story. This helps sustain a sense of the time-based nature of musical form, and can give improvisation an emotional structure.

Listening led

This kind of music-making involves a specifically aural imagination or aural responses, and sometimes develops later than we might expect. There may be a focus on particular aspects of sound – timbre, pitch and melody, rhythm and dynamic – in any combination. Even from early stages, individual pupils are often more aurally aware of some aspects of music than they are of others. By drawing on these differences, group teaching can be effective in raising the aural sensitivity of everyone involved.

Technology led

The use of technology – computers, keyboards, karaoke, phones (even toy versions of these things) and electronic games – can stimulate inventive music-making that offers access at all levels and in different formats, from devices that require little technical or musical knowledge to specialist computer software. Technology also offers students opportunities to:

- work beyond their performing capability;
- explore sonorities;
- engage in creative processes structured by software or presentation;
- compose or arrange music for many players by building up a layer at a time.

Music technology in practice

p. 72

Many young people already enjoy music through technology and find it accessible regardless of their theoretical understanding (which they build as they go along). Pupils can bring their experience to the group and use technology to support recording, composing, arranging and notating.

Creative starting points

This section contains deliberately open-ended starter activities to enable pupils to respond in their own ways, according to their own understanding. These give teachers opportunities to listen to and observe a whole range of creative responses.

One-note improvisations

Use one pitch or, if more appropriate, one timbre. For example, ask pupils to play any of the following:

- an 'easy' note or sound (one that can be found and played without difficulty);
- the note A, then B, then C (work alphabetically);
- the group's 'best' note or timbre (discuss the choice with the group);
- a newly learnt note, timbre or articulation (to help pupils get used to a fingering or technique).

Then use this note for any or all of the following activities:

- Each member of the group plays the note for four straight beats. Try to move from one player to the next as steadily and evenly as possible, as if only one person is playing. (Develop this by varying the number of beats. Then ask pupils to work out ways of varying their turn. Discuss and try out possibilities.)
- Each member of the group plays in turn (for an unspecified length of time). As soon as one player stops, the next picks up. (Develop this by asking pupils to listen and decide on possible 'rules' for following on: try to copy the last player; try to do something opposite; focus on rhythm; focus on dynamics; build up tempo; build up dynamics.)
- Use a keyboard (live or preset accompaniment), guitar, percussion (a simple drum or tambourine beat will do), drum machine, mobile phone, or recorded backing. Take turns to improvise against this, keeping in time. It works well if the backing has some change in it – for example, two bars with a chord shift per bar, or a percussion beat with a change of timbre. (Or see 'One Note Rhythm Games', in Duckett and Price, *Explorations*.) Give pupils plenty of time to absorb the feel of the backing. (Develop this by building up, so that each player takes a longer turn. Vary the speed or style of the backing and adapt the improvisations accordingly. Insert a group riff as a backing from which individuals then depart; invent a recurring motif, with opportunities for solos.)

These activities provide a secure starting point and are appropriate for players of varying levels of skill, enabling them to work together. Repeat the activities, engaging the group in discussion, making suggestions and trying things out. Do not try to tidy the result into a neat musical format too soon. If performers have difficulty coming in on cue, accommodate this by slowing down, leaving leeway or gaps. Expect all players to adapt to each person's capabilities by listening.

Made as played

Ask group members to make up a new piece, tune or starting pattern at home, to bring to the next lesson. They can do this by doodling and finding something that sounds interesting, but they have to be able to play it in class for others to copy or learn – writing it down is optional. Try to get at least one volunteer, then continue to offer opportunities so that everyone starts bringing their own music. If anyone remains reluctant, make more specific requests like 'Would you make us a tune to practise this new note (or sound, or rhythm)? Nothing too hard and not very long.' Ask for and listen to all offerings at subsequent lessons. Encourage pupils to:

- play or learn each other's music, however rudimentary;
- suggest ideas for further new music;
- continue to bring their own pieces or ideas to class.

This request will launch the kind of composing that is likely to be going on under cover anyway (Glover, *Children Composing*, p. 77). The resulting music will probably be concerned with the physical movements and musical scope associated with the instrument in the learner's experience so far. It often promotes a need for further technique or extension of what has been learnt – pursuing this will improve both technical capability and creativity. To develop quality and confidence, establish a group ethos of listening attentively to all contributions and of describing rather than judging them. This links with the 'Listening and Internalising Area' in *A Common Approach 2002*, as an ideal opportunity for pupils to:

- listen to music with concentration;
- have a clear aural perception of the music to be played or sung;
- recognize and discriminate between musical elements;
- recognize and convey structural elements in their playing or singing.

Making arrangements

The process of interpretation forms the basis for developing arranging skills. Select any short solo piece currently in the group's repertoire and ask each pupil to bring to the next session some suggestions as to how it might be performed by the group. Set up an expectation of some thinking and experimentation, independent of work in the lesson. Remind pupils of the possibilities available, considering different musical aspects (tempo, dynamics, timbre, phrasing, balance and accompaniment), as well as instrumental factors such as breathing, tonguing, bowing, plucking, strumming, damping, and sticking. These will, of course, relate to their level of experience. Over time, try out pupils' suggestions. In each case:

- ask the student to coach the group in how to perform;
- perform and record the performances;

- listen, and discuss how the music takes on different guises as a result of each pupil's suggestions;
- encourage a range of preferences across the group as to what works well.

Pupils can work in pairs or individually on this, and the scope of the activity can range from a simple plan for dynamics or expressive interpretation to a full-scale arrangement. Make sure each version is someone's full responsibility, so that it amounts to more than just one 'committee' arrangement.

As with all pupil-led activities, this provides a useful window for the teacher on to the way pupils understand, think about, and respond to the music they play. It is worth taking plenty of time over this, perhaps running it across half a term's lessons. This allows ideas to gather momentum from week to week, and pupils to develop their ideas through listening to their own and others' work. A useful development is to perform or listen to two versions of any repertoire piece and play 'Spot the difference'. Even if pupils lack the vocabulary to describe differences, they begin to sense how much performers' choices affect the musical outcome.

I encourage the introduction of scoring – the concept of how sounds mix and work together. There is a necessary level of arrangement required to revoice and rescore existing group activities. This is actually a constant and live activity through any group session. It is important to have many options available, to keep the group session as an emerging canvas and to present the possibility of what this group can do to make this activity its own. PC

Moving further into full arranging might start by asking two players to experiment with ways of arranging a piece between them. They might play alternate phrases; alternate between playing together and individually; or invent an additional instrumental line, rhythmic accompaniment, drone, ostinato, bass or chord pattern, percussion part or counter-rhythm. More simply, some might work on adding an introduction or a coda.

Picture–word

Using visual and literary stimuli can be particularly effective in encouraging pupils to explore the boundaries of sound on their instrument. Use words and illustrations that imply a mood, emotion or state of mind. The following categories provide some starting points:

- animals (such as dolphins leaping, swans gliding);
- fiction and fantasy (such as wizards casting spells, aliens landing on the moon);
- sports and games (such as trampolining, kite-flying);
- nature and the weather (such as a sunrise, snowflakes, lightning);
- transport (such as a motorbike in traffic, a helicopter taking off).

> Free improvisation using sound effects and a story is quite popular with some younger players. I have found that this works better in larger groups as the children are generally less inhibited about sounding like a ghost, or whatever, when lots of people are doing the same. A structure helps, and inviting the children to put forward their ideas about what could be a good beginning or ending, for example, is always interesting. Lots of technical points can be worked into this kind of thing.
>
> KB

Or you may wish to use individual words expressing emotions, moods or states of mind directly (confused, nervous, serene…); or an activity word (bouncing, swaying…). Timbral exploration of the instrument through extended techniques alerts pupils to the variety of sound production and articulation possibilities on their instrument.

Building improvising skills

Over time introduce the group to a series of basic improvising frameworks, such as those suggested below. Revisit the frameworks as long as pupils are motivated. Before they start being really inventive within any structure, performers need plenty of familiarity with the possibilities and the sensation of creating. Build up the different frameworks as a repertoire, just as you would build a set of pieces.

Taking turns

Just taking turns to play is an excellent launch into improvisation. 'Shall I start or will you?' can be enough introduction for early explorations; the most positive approach is to do this without any preconception or judgement of results. Whether between teacher and pupil or two pupils, the music is likely to include both routine patterns that arise from fingerwork, bowing or embouchure and some character, rhythmic life and creative exploration. The aim is to enable pupils to use their ears, inner musical sense and personality together.

Call and response

Improvise all together, in response to a leader's 'call'. Do not worry if responses are incompatible. Enjoy the drama of a lone voice answered by energetic cacophony. (There is safety in numbers to start with – pupils can try things out without feeling conspicuous.) Continue by:

- responding in threes, twos and then solo;
- having two or three turns per pupil (using the same or different responses), then just one (which requires greater cueing skill and quicker thinking);

- varying the call (played by teacher or pupil);
- taking an idea from a pupil's response and using it as a call (this encourages and endorses musical value).

Exploring musical materials and structures

Here a musical starting point is introduced, tried out, and listened to. Its feel and possibilities are discussed. The framework for improvisation is the 'rule' or boundaries of working with the chosen musical materials. Starting points could include:

- an agreed note set, scale or mode;
- a dance rhythm;
- a contrast (such as different registers, dynamics, timbres or techniques).

> Sometimes as a group activity we make an instant folksong using a pentatonic scale. We start by playing the scale. Then each pupil plays a phrase, to be answered by the next in turn. It is also possible to set up a drone-type accompaniment to support the instant folksong.
>
> RPe

Accompaniments and backing tracks

Improvising to an accompaniment or backing introduces another experience for learners in which they must become aware of a basic framework and find ways to work with or against it. Whether the accompaniment is a fixed, repeating idea or something more flexible, the performer has to try to work within boundaries of timing, rhythm, note set, or harmony. But improvising is in itself a way of exploring these boundaries and discovering different kinds of potential within them. Backing tracks are particularly useful for introducing or reinforcing new scale patterns and instrumental techniques, and they enable pupils to work with musical styles that may be difficult to introduce in other ways. For older pupils, more adult forms – such as blues, jazz and folk – will be appealing.

> Improvisation is the life-blood of any group session, but it needs to be managed in a highly structured and organized framework. One big danger in a percussion group is the natural tendency for the session to become a free-for-all. Backing tracks are a useful way of holding everything together – if improvisation happens then it has a purposeful context. Improvisation carries with it responsibility to other members of the group.
>
> PC

For teachers whose time is too limited to create tracks themselves, liaison with schools or students can usually provide access to ready-made backings. Many

Music technology in practice

p. 72

classroom music resources include accompaniments and backing tracks on CD; schools and music centres may have these to hand. Pre-recorded backings can usually be found on keyboards or drum machines. Computers are readily available to many children, who will relish the opportunity to create music using sequencing or notation software. Pupils may well be able to create something independently, or in class music lessons, for use in the group.

Set up a simple chord progression and let pupils listen in for a while before doing anything. Try:

- improvising with voices (even *sotto voce*);
- improvising with instruments (using just a few notes to begin with);
- student and teacher taking turns to model ideas and help build the music;
- repeating ideas to focus on how they sound musically;
- exploring different moods and styles with the same progression.

Composing

Children have an enormous capacity to produce individual compositions. Composing thrives in group learning situations because a community of musicians provides:

- listeners, and the experience of listening to other people's new music;
- a rich environment for exchanging ideas and sparking creativity;
- other performers to compose for, so that both group and solo music can be composed, tried out and kept in the repertoire;
- an understanding of how instruments sound together, of different players' capabilities, of how musical roles can be shared (such as foreground and accompaniment, melody and bass, and so on), and of how musical drama unfolds.

Composing thrives when viewed as an intrinsic aspect of instrumental learning. Learning an instrument includes understanding what it can do, learning to exploit its possibilities and contributing actively to its musical repertoire. The following can build on the starting points and improvisation outlined above.

Composing in pairs

Pair up pupils and ask them each to compose (by doodling or improvising) something for the other to play. If they like, they can do this out of lesson time so that ideas are tried out before being shared with the group. You might encourage pupils to interview each other to find out what notes they know, what they can or cannot do, and what kind of music they might enjoy playing. This works best if pupils with roughly similar abilities work together. The aim is that pupils at least consider someone else's technical capabilities and also their personality and tastes.

Imagine a beginning

This approach is based in learning to use aural imagination. It can be used as a way into composing for even very inexperienced players. Warm up by asking each person in the group to practise (all at once, in cacophony) a short phrase or motif. This might be a melodic or rhythmic idea, or a timbre or effect (such as short sounds, a slow slide, a trill that starts slowly and speeds up).

Make a really focused 'listening silence'. Let each player in turn play his or her motif and then leave a silence while the rest 'think it'. Then follow this sequence:

- practise 'hear it and then think it' around the group several times;
- ask pupils to try to 'think' one of the motifs or a new one, imagining the music;
- ask pupils to think a motif and then play it, or to describe a motif and ask someone else to play it.

Then ask everyone to close their eyes, clear their minds of sound and listen for an idea that could be the beginning of a new piece for a solo instrument. It can help to imagine an empty stage, silence, a spotlight on the player, and so on. Try out these ideas and discuss how each might lead into a new composition. Let pupils try to develop a new composition from their starting idea, away from the lesson.

Composing challenge

The previous activity started with a detail and developed it, whereas this starts with the outline. Pupils set a challenge, for themselves or each other, consisting of a verbal outline for some music. For example:

- 'Make a piece that starts low and slow and gradually winds higher and faster.'
- 'Make a piece to send someone to sleep.'

Pupils take the challenge away, then bring their ideas, finished or unfinished, to share with the group.

Choose a memorable phrase from a song being studied. Ask the pupils to compose a short song based on that phrase.

More advanced pupils may wish to try and compose a short unaccompanied piece for the voices in the group. This could be with or without words. Encourage pupils to use devices such as repetition or sequence and incorporate some dynamic variations. They could record their work on tape or write it down using conventional or pattern notation.

HP

Journeys

Using journeys as the basis for composition is a good way of tapping into children's imagination. Like music, a journey is sequential, and the language of travel provides a set of useful metaphors for music (Odam, *Sounding Symbol*, p. 67). Children can invent their own journey narrative, drawing on everyday or imaginary scenarios, and use this as a structural framework for a piece of music. The teacher's role here is to encourage pupils to make sure their piece is musically coherent, and to avoid over-literalism or simple sound effects.

Borrowing

Composing is always enriched by listening to other people's music. Without trying to imitate other composers' work fully, borrowing an idea or approach can be a good starting point. This might begin from listening to a piece that has some obvious features – a melody with big leaps, walls of sound interspersed with silence, echo effects, a rhythmic ostinato. Ask pupils how they think the composer made up the music. For example:

- What decision did the composer make first?
- Which musical ideas came first?
- How have the ideas been developed?
- What difficulties might there have been?
- What effect did the composer intend the music to have on an audience?

This insists on pupils listening from the composer's point of view as well as from the listener's. Ask pupils to each choose a musical idea from the piece, to use as the basis for their own music.

Capturing compositions

Pupils remember their improvisations and recall them as 'pieces' or parts of pieces. Individual ideas can be brought together in a group composition. From there it is a short step to using manuscript paper to store the ideas. By using notes they are familiar with, they will know what they look like and enjoy writing them out themselves, using printed examples as a reference.   RW/RC

There are many ways in which pupils can capture or set down their compositions – for example, some pupils may be comfortable with graphic notation, some with manuscript paper and others with recording equipment or computer software. The principal aim is to encourage pupils to make some kind of record of their work for future performance or other reference: teachers need to be flexible in their approach to this, and encourage a variety of strategies. You may find that some pupils already keep a composing notebook or audio diary of their work. Finding connections with pupils' current classroom activities may help to get the balance right.

Notation can, of course, take many different forms and can function in different ways: as a mental map for the composer, a set of technical instructions for performers, or a framework for improvisation. Graphic notation can be a useful way to introduce musical concepts and can provide a basis for discussing how aural and visual elements interact. It is not necessarily a vague way of representing sound – in fact it may be a very precise set of instructions and may cover elements, such as timbre, for which staff notation has no equivalent. Some computer programs, such as Morton Subotnick's *Making Music*, offer graphic-score tools, which may already be familiar to pupils.

There is a danger that if too much emphasis is given to the manipulation of staff notation then creativity is diminished, as the ability of children to compose music usually far exceeds their ability to notate it. Nevertheless, learning the basics of how to score music effectively and using the appropriate conventions is an important composing tool and one that reinforces pupils' developing musical literacy. The necessity of visual clarity and the usefulness of numbering bars or giving cues, for example, becomes self-evident when music is being rehearsed or performed with the group.

Evaluating outcomes

The key to all evaluation of improvising, composing and arranging is learning to listen skilfully. It is necessary to shed preconceptions, hear what is present in the music (as opposed to what is absent), and to understand how learners handle different musical elements at different levels of experience. It is useful to bear in mind the distinction between assessing pupils' skills, knowledge development and understanding, and evaluating the musical outcomes and products themselves.

It is important, however, to engage in formative assessment with pupils and to give feedback. Teachers need to make the learning content of activities explicit by outlining objectives and aims clearly. Feedback can then be given using the same vocabulary, expressed in relation to the stated objectives. Asking children to review and assess their own work on the same basis will encourage real learning and engagement, with the teacher reinforcing this and eliciting helpful comments from other children.

Formative assessment strategies

p. 119

When responding to musical outcomes, it is often useful to comment first in descriptive terms: 'I heard the music start slowly and low in pitch, then gradually speed up.' This helps pupils understand how others hear their work, and models ways of talking about the music itself. Value judgements can follow later, but must be carefully thought through. Teachers need to be clear what pupils will do with judgements of personal taste. A remark such as 'I like that very much' may be welcome, but may equally be irrelevant. Moreover, it only has value if someone is also prepared to say 'I don't like that at all', which is probably unhelpful for other reasons. Similarly, a comment such as 'That was a good beginning' is of little use unless it is clear what 'good' is based on; 'That beginning made me want to know what happens next' imparts more valuable information. 'How can you make that better?' can also be a two-edged sword, since most of us would have made it better if we had known how. Successful evaluation requires discussing evaluative criteria with pupils and agreeing on a set of criteria that everyone can understand, perceive and apply. Discussion can then be based on listening, and reasons can be given for any comments made.

Feedback in a group context

p. 124 ➡

No one can begin improvising and composing if the outcome has to be 'good' from the start. Mistakes are part of the process; recovery mechanisms can only be developed if this is openly acknowledged. Mistakes can act as the catalyst for creativity, so risk-taking should not be discouraged – indeed, it informs all creativity. The teacher should also make mistakes and show that in this context it does not matter. High standards come from being willing to try, listen and improve, not from anxiety as to whether what is produced is good enough, right or wrong.

The creative group

Motivation soars when pupils know they belong to a musical network where it is safe to contribute their own ideas, to try things out, to play with music, to communicate musically with other people and to bring their own music for others to play or comment on. Much of this activity provides opportunities to practise, consolidate technique and deepen musical understanding.

The aim must be to develop musicians who are technically proficient, where 'technique' is not abstract but applied at every level – in short, they should be able to:

- get the sound they want;
- create the musical meaning they want;
- lead or follow, interact and communicate effectively with others in all kinds of performing roles and situations;
- understand and interpret their own and others' music with a sense of style that goes beyond just playing notes.

A teaching approach that enables creative musical activity to remain intrinsic to instrumental learning draws on the musical energy that probably brought the learner to music lessons in the first place. Within this approach, pupils learn to explore and use their own musical voice and to hear and respect the musical voices of others.

9

The psychology of group teaching and learning

Lucinda Mackworth-Young

Can you remember how you felt on your way to your first music lesson with a new teacher, or on your way to a new class or group? What did you hope for, need, or fear, both from the teacher and from the group? Think of your conscious, rational feelings and your deep, non-rational feelings.

Any new situation brings both excitement and anxiety. As a rule, the older the pupil, the more anxiety there will be. This may be anxiety about finding the teaching room, being late, whether the teacher or group will be welcoming, whether the teacher will think the pupil is any good, and what the other pupils will be like. There is a need to feel safe and accepted by both the teacher and the group. Without this, pupils cannot easily learn: learning requires them to be open to new experiences and to risk trying new things (and failing). Extreme anxiety can cause pupils to feel helpless and overwhelmed, as though they are falling apart. Common signs of learning anxiety are:

- evading lessons or practice (it feels better not to try than to try and fail);
- arriving late for lessons, or making excuses to leave early;
- engaging the teacher or other group members in distracting chatter;
- switching off – being unable to hear or understand what is being said;
- racing ahead out of control;
- tears or other evidence of distress.

There are many practical activities that can relieve anxiety in a group situation. These include name games (particularly useful at the start of a new group), rhythm games, pitch games, singing games, theory games (using board and dice); clapping, stepping, moving; improvising and playing by ear (so long as the activities are properly within the pupils' grasp). These involve pupils aurally, kinaesthetically, intellectually and with their whole bodies in such a way that they are more likely to be emotionally engaged and 'present' in their learning.

Transferring the role of parent on to the teacher

Pupils (at any age) easily key into childhood and infantile feelings of terror and helplessness in the face of being lost or unable to succeed. They instinctively transfer a parental role on to the teacher, needing the teacher to hold them safe and believe in their potential. Seen from this perspective, it is easy to understand why the teacher's care and approval, or neglect and disapproval, can feel like a matter of life or death. It is also easy to appreciate that within group lessons there may be sibling rivalry. Each pupil needs to feel special to the teacher; some need to feel that no one else in the group is more special than they are. So pupils tend to compete with each other for the teacher's attention and praise.

Child protection

p. 134 →

Internalizations, inner resource and projection

The extent to which pupils can remain present and engaged in learning – especially when the going gets tough – and the extent to which they can hear and trust the teacher depends largely on what they are already saying to themselves, inside their own heads. It depends on their internalizations and resulting inner resource. Pupils who have heard, internalized and so say to themselves 'You are clever! You can succeed!' are more likely to keep trying when faced with difficulty than those who say to themselves 'You'll never be able to do this, the others are much better than you.' Moreover, through the projection of their internalizations, what pupils hear from us depends upon what they are already saying to themselves. That is why some pupils are relaxed, smiling and sure of our appreciation, while others are tense, worried and able to hear only criticism, whether or not we have said a word!

By the time pupils come to us for lessons they will have developed a variety of habitual patterns of behaviour formed from their internalizations, and as defence mechanisms against their anxiety about not being able to succeed. Such behaviour patterns can hamper both the pupil's ability to learn and the smooth running of the group. In addition to the signs of anxiety described above they include:

- having no idea how to be a good pupil (having no such example from home and insufficient social skill to pick it up from school);
- resisting anything new;
- habitually doing as little as possible;
- being quiet in order not to be noticed (thus avoiding the risk of being exposed as unable to do something);

- being disruptive in order to attract attention;
- being disruptive in order to divert attention from inner pain and anxiety;
- being nastily competitive, putting down others in the group, scapegoating (unconsciously projecting individual feelings of inferiority on to peers, and then punishing peers for the perceived inferiority).

It is always helpful for us to remember that our pupils' behaviour, especially at the beginning, often says much more about them, their internalizations and habitual patterns than it does about us and our teaching.

There are ways of working with a group to deal with issues of internalization and projection, and to bolster individuals' inner resource. Most importantly, foster mutual support. Encourage pupils to feel and say positive things about each other's efforts and playing. There could even be a rule (which you can turn into a game) that pupils are not allowed even to think – much less say – anything negative.

Understanding learning

Can you now remember how you learnt? Were you taught step by step, methodically? Holistically and intuitively? Pupils learn through total immersion and interaction with learning materials, using all of their senses and faculties. They learn using both hemispheres of the brain, and they learn aurally, kinaesthetically, visually, intellectually and with their whole bodies. Through these means they build up their own internal structure of concepts and skills, linking each new concept or skill into a pre-existing internal structure. It is this internal structure which constitutes their learning.

Left-brain (logical) skills are methodical and analytical, proceeding step by step. They are excellent for learning technical skills and note reading, and for containing and framing tasks into clear, achievable bite-sized pieces. Most teaching is left-brained.

Right-brain (*gestalt* – or 'seeing the whole') skills are intuitive, holistic, symbolic and are excellent for lifting the music off the written page. They include:

- feeling ('What do you feel in this piece? Try making it mysterious; see how that feels');
- imagination ('What picture does it conjure in your mind?');
- metaphor ('Try making the tremolo shimmer like a heat haze in the desert');
- humour (making light of mishaps and difficulties).

Many group musical activities – because they are often practical and physical, involving interaction – tend to be right-brained, generating a very 'present' energy. Most practice is right-brained, as the left-brained approach, though palatable in the lesson with the teacher, can feel arid and dry when pupils are practising alone. However, the 'let's start at the beginning and finish at the end to see how it goes', right-brained approach to practice, so common with so many pupils, rarely enables their performance to withstand the slight pressure of playing to the teacher, let alone the greater pressure of a more formal performance. 'It went all right at home' is the familiar cry!

In order for playing to be secure, pupils need to know the music consciously in every way:

Aurally Do pupils know the sound of the melody? The bass line? The inner parts? Can they sing them? Group singing and playing activities help aural perception.

Kinaesthetically Do pupils know how every physical movement feels? In order to feel deeply secure physically, keyboard players need to practise with the sound turned off, wind players need to practise without blowing, string players without bowing. And as the right side of the brain operates the left side of the body, and vice versa, it is better still if everyone practises hands separately with and without sound (as appropriate for the instrument).

Intellectually and visually Do pupils understand everything on the written page? Can they see the shapes and patterns their fingers make on the instrument? Can they visualize themselves playing, inwardly hearing the music, inwardly feeling the physical sensation and, if learning from memory, inwardly seeing the notes they are playing on the instrument?

These skills need to be practised at a speed where pupils feel comfortably in control rather than hoping for the best! Interestingly, singing the counts ('one, two and three', for example) while playing (or while fingering, without blowing, on wind instruments) is perhaps the most effective way to bring conscious and deep control to playing, as it requires a particular connection between the hemispheres of the brain and effectively integrates all the necessary skills.

'Whole body' For added security and musical appreciation, pupils can internalize pulse, rhythm, pitch and phrasing using 'whole body' skills like walking, dancing and gesturing as appropriate.

Pupils with learning difficulties

A word for those teaching pupils with learning difficulties: our current conventional system is note-reading based, demanding an eye–finger link, so any pupils who are naturally ear–finger orientated, or who have a weak eye–finger link, will be disadvantaged. These pupils could include dyslexics (for whom written symbols tend not to stay still), dyspraxics (who have difficulty sequencing) and those with lesser intellectual capacity (including Downs Syndrome pupils) for whom the written page is simply another block between them and the music. For all, but especially for these pupils, we must remember that making music is what counts, and that playing by ear and improvising are likely to be their preferred activities. Whole-body activities like clapping, stepping and dancing can be immensely helpful here, too.

Creating and directing energy in group lessons

Bring to mind a recent music lesson that went very well. What made it so successful? Think about the quality and direction of energy between teacher and pupils, and the material being taught. The chances are that there was a mutual flow of positive energy between teacher and pupils in this lesson, and positive emotional engagement with the material being learnt – both interest in it and a feeling of being able to succeed with it. Positive emotional energy is the key. By monitoring your own feelings, you can be aware of the quality of energy – or feeling – in the group because feelings, whether of anxiety, frustration and boredom or excitement, appreciation and magic, are conveyed gut to gut, bypassing reason. So if you find yourself feeling any emotion, particularly any negative emotion, perhaps uncertainty or inferiority – 'I'll never be able to teach this, he must be thinking I'm a useless teacher' – consider the possibility that it might be the pupils who are thinking 'I'll never be able to learn this, she must be thinking I'm useless.' Then, because they are felt mutually, the simplest way to resolve these feelings is to give to the pupils what you feel you need yourself – reassurance, appreciation and a shift in activity.

Matching work to pupils' ability

◀ p. 61

Tasks that are too difficult or too easy both produce negative energy, so make sure that the group is appropriately challenged: in a group situation this often means having more than one activity happening at once. For example, while the teacher is attending to one or two pupils, other pupils could be:

- quietly exploring new music or a new skill (silently visualizing or fingering it through);
- teaching each other (teaching helps deepen understanding; teaching is learning);
- working out an improvisation;
- preparing a graphic-notation score;
- completing a theory worksheet.

Be aware too of the direction of energy between the teacher and the group. If you are being too directive – and the pupils are not responding – you may feel frustrated, blocked and exhausted; and the pupils may be feeling forced down a route they do not want to take at a speed they are not able to go. If this happens it can help to hand over temporarily to the pupils, asking them what they would like to play, or whether they can identify and suggest ways to handle the difficulty. But if you are not being directive enough, you may feel boredom or lack of control; likewise the pupils may feel anxious, lost and even abandoned (also possibly angry with the teacher for allowing this situation). In this case, take more charge, change the activity to something the pupils enjoy and can do, or redefine the task so that pupils can manage it.

Involve pupils as much as possible in a democratic process (as appropriate to their ages and stages and in line with their personal ambitions), helping them decide together what they should learn, in time for which goals, how they are doing as they are learning, what to practise and what the rules of behaviour are. In this way pupils feel an intrinsic and responsible part of the process and the group, and so they invest more energy in its success.

Disruptive behaviour

Make pupils aware of their behaviour (which is usually unconscious and reactive rather than active) by reflecting it back to them gently as an observation ('Sam, it seems you need all the attention today'). Then, once pupils are conscious of their behaviour, they can decide what to do about it. In the majority of cases, individuals will want to fall in line with the rest of the group. In conclusion, here are a few strategies which will help to minimize the effects of disruptive behaviour.

Teach positively
Leave pupils in no doubt that they can succeed by pointing out that they have already done so. For instance: 'That note was beautifully articulated. Now articulate these ones as well.' Or: 'Jason is sitting ready' (which alerts the others to do the same).

Use the naturally competitive element

A pupil is not likely to want to be the only one who 'can't do it' or who lets the group down – and so may be more easily persuaded to participate or practise simply by being part of a group.

Use criticism with care

Feedback in a group context

p. 124 →

Criticism can create anxiety, and anxiety blocks unless it drives. For instance, it may be helpful to criticize pupils to make them feel *more* anxious about coming to the next lesson without having practised than about facing the practice itself. But this only works if the relationship is sufficiently strong and pupils believe they can succeed, so that they want to work to regain the temporarily lost approval. Otherwise they will experience criticism as an attack (particularly if they feel shown up in front of the group) and may defend themselves by giving up.

Make success a priority

Make sure pupils succeed in the lesson because they practise when they *can* play it, don't they? And 'visible' successes like concerts or exams are motivating and rewarding for both pupils and their parents.

Encourage independence

Teach pupils to teach themselves and help them to use their own inner resource so that, in time, the pupil–teacher relationship is more adult-to-adult than child-to-parent.

10

Practice

Carole Jenner-Timms

Practice is necessary for any progress to be made in instrumental or vocal learning. According to the *Concise Oxford Dictionary*, 'practice' means 'a repeated exercise in an activity requiring the development of skill' or 'a session of this'. It is important that pupils do not regard their practice as a boring chore: teachers have a responsibility to make it as interesting and productive as possible. As pupils progress, effective practice will ensure independent learning as long as skills, knowledge and understanding are integral to music-making.

Teaching practice skills

If pupils are to practise effectively they must be able to answer the following three questions:

- What tasks do I need to practise?
- Why do I need to practise these tasks?
- How am I going to practise them?

A group lesson is an ideal set-up for pupils to discuss these questions, even in the relatively early stages. As a result of these discussions, pupils will have ownership of their learning and will become more critically aware; consequently they will become more 'intrinsically' motivated. Questioning in a group lesson can open up useful opportunities for pupils to discuss together their understanding of aural, cognitive, musical, performance and technical skills. Pupils can be encouraged to make informed decisions and have opinions about their efforts. This can have a profound influence on their playing and practice away from the lesson and helps them to become independent learners.

Motivation

p. 108 ➤

Practice tasks must be meaningful. They must relate to the teacher's long- and short-term planning, and pupils need to see and understand the relevance of what they are being asked to practise. Teachers are responsible for showing pupils the connection between lesson objectives and homework tasks, as well as for creating opportunities for group discussion on how best to practise them. And teachers need to help pupils to understand the aural, visual and kinaesthetic forms of learning so that they can reflect and question themselves on their practice efforts. This is again possible from the early stages of learning.

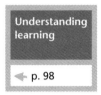

p. 98

Tips for practising could include:

- concentrate when practising;
- relax and practise slowly;
- do not let the music be boring;
- work on things you cannot do;
- play everything as if you are singing – always make your best sound;
- learn from your mistakes;
- look for connections with other things you have learnt about music.

You could ask group members to share and evaluate other practice tips.

How much practice and how often?

Regular practice is essential for progress to be made. Little and often is certainly more effective than one long practice session the evening before the next lesson. Teachers have differing views on the number of recommended practice sessions a week, but it is generally accepted that in the early stages 10 to 15 minutes a day will promote the ready retention of skills, knowledge and understanding. Practice time can gradually be increased according to the pupils' progress but consideration must be given to the differing physical demands of instruments, as well as to pupils' varying powers of concentration. Some pupils, particularly younger ones, like to identify a regular practice time each day. This could be a topic for discussion within the group.

The practice environment

Ideally, practice sessions need to take place in a quiet, light and airy environment away from distraction. In a group lesson the teacher can lead a discussion on the best environment for practice. The following questions need to be asked:

- Where do pupils practise?
- Do pupils have a music stand at home?
- Do pupils understand why the use of a music stand is necessary in order to nurture good habits of posture (for string, brass and wind players)?

- Do pupils practise in a quiet environment? If not, what distractions are there?
- Does anyone listen to their practice? If yes, is it helpful, or not?

How will pupils know what to practise?

Practice targets do need to be written down in some form. For primary-age pupils, practice diaries which provide space for both parent and teacher comments are ideal. Sometimes, however, this method is difficult for those teaching several pupils in a group for a relatively short time – more time could be spent writing than teaching! If tutor books are used, then it may be enough to write a date by the side of the exercises to be practised, with concise reminders of specific details pertinent to the pupil concerned (these could be written on small pieces of removable sticky paper). Most secondary-age pupils have a 'contact' type of notebook for general school use. This can also be used for pupils to write details of their practice that can easily be dictated by the teacher in the closing moments of a lesson.

Pupils should not leave a lesson without having a clear idea of what they need to do before the next lesson. They should be reminded that practice does not 'make perfect'; it only 'makes permanent'. In other words, practising badly will only cement bad habits and therefore be a waste of time. It could even be argued that, while it is important to establish a practice culture, it is better not to practise at all than habitually to play for any length of time, unsupervised, with the wrong hand positions or finger movements. Practice diaries are indispensable in that, as far as possible, both pupils and parents understand exactly what needs practising and how it should be practised. It helps if diaries have a place where parents can make comments and ask questions.   RW/RC

How best to plan practice?

3

Developing technical skills

Practice targets must be relevant to the teaching that has taken place in the lesson. For example, if a warm-up procedure is used in the lesson, warm-ups should also be encouraged in practice at home. Pupils must therefore understand the purpose of these exercises. Technical exercises should obviously be practised in between lessons if pupils are to develop their technique. Again, they need to understand why these exercises are necessary and to be taught how to question themselves intuitively about their efforts when they practise away from the lesson.

Encourage the pupils within the group to keep a diary of things to be practised and studied throughout the week. They might also like to write down how the practice went and report back in the next lesson any difficulties or triumphs.   HP

Teachers should try to find studies and pieces that are relevant and appropriate for their pupils' technical ability but, at the same time, are not too difficult. If pupils are learning pieces within their technical ability, then musical issues can be far more easily understood. (During lessons teachers should constantly assess pupils' ability to read notation to ensure they have an adequate level of understanding for their practice away from the lesson.) Where possible, integrate different elements of the practice so that one individual task gives focus and purpose to another. For example, pupils will be far more likely to practise scales and arpeggios if they are in the same key as the piece they are studying. Pupils will then see the relevance of what they are being asked to do – at this point, they start to analyse phrases and make musical connections, and practice takes on its own momentum.

You can use the group dynamic to encourage practice, too. Scales and arpeggios can be played very enjoyably during a group lesson. Scales can be played as a round with each pupil starting two notes (a 3rd) apart and arpeggios one note apart. Ensemble scale books that provide more ideas are also available in music shops. As a group lesson offers a wonderful opportunity to incorporate ensemble playing and singing, pupils can be encouraged to practise individual parts at home so that ensemble skills can be addressed in the lesson. The idea of 'practising a part' is good training for lifelong music-making and also helps to foster independent learning.

Apart from warm-ups and technical exercises, scales and arpeggios, studies, pieces and ensemble parts, pupils should be encouraged to practise sight-reading, and to play things for fun, whether it be pop tunes or pieces they have previously played and enjoyed. Playing for pleasure is an important factor in the development of pupils' enthusiasm. Games and exploring are also vital elements of practice. For example, suggest pupils play well-known tunes by ear; imagine (and play) new music; take a tune they already know but start it on a different note and continue to play it for as long as possible; or play a piece backwards. All these things make pupils think about music and make them listen critically; but, above all, they are enjoyable.

Playing by ear

← p. 81

Problem-solving

Teachers have a responsibility to help pupils solve problems that they encounter in both playing and practice, and to demonstrate that practice and problem-solving can be rewarding. Problem-solving during practice stems from effective teaching strategies used in lessons. There is no harm in using a 'practice' teaching style in a group lesson when, for a few moments, pupils are let loose on a technical task or musical phrase. The problems encountered by pupils can then be discussed, and ideas for improvement put forward by teacher and pupils alike. Pupils should be encouraged to use their critical awareness to answer the following questions:

- What is the problem?
- Where is the problem?
- Why does the problem occur?
- How can the problem be solved?

These questions require the use of visual, aural and kinaesthetic learning and analytical skills. Only when these four questions are answered can problems be solved and effective practice take place. Once pupils have identified problems, they need to be equipped with strategies to solve them. Some of these are given below.

- To improve technical and reading skills, appropriate sections or bars can be identified to be played repeatedly and with a metronome to aid time-keeping.
- Pupils can produce a well-projected sound, combined with effective articulation and accurate intonation, only if they have sufficient aural memories of their teacher's modelling. For this reason, it is important to let pupils hear your playing, as well as the other way round.
- Posture problems can be remodelled at home, particularly if the pupil and teacher have looked at the issues in the lesson using a mirror. Pupils can be encouraged to eliminate points of tension, particularly if they are questioned effectively and regularly in lessons about habits of posture and, if appropriate, embouchure. Group teaching offers the opportunity for pupils to compare posture and embouchure, and the associated muscular movements, and to discuss their reactions, so that their practice will be more effective.

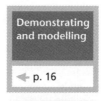

Demonstrating and modelling

← p. 16

Posture

← p. 28

- In order to enable pupils to make interpretative decisions, teachers should identify exercises to be played:

    a) with different dynamic levels (including crescendo and diminuendo);
    b) with different articulations (for example, staccato, sostenuto, legato, marcato, and so on);
    c) in different moods (for example, happy, sad, fast, slow, rushing, plodding along).

- Encouraging pupils to memorize phrases so that they are free from technical hitches creates space to concentrate on shaping, expression and fluency. Singing phrases aids internalization. Transposition of phrases into different keys aids aural and key awareness.

- To encourage a creative approach to practice, teachers could create exercises to develop certain aspects of technique. This can start as a group activity. Pupils can then be encouraged to make up their own exercises at home and notate them. Improvisation, using the theme of a piece as a starting point, could be worked on as a group activity and continued for homework.

- The use of CD backing-tracks can make practice more interesting too. There are many examples of music in different styles available nowadays. Some tutor books also provide CD accompaniments and examples to enhance musical understanding.

- Finally, pupils can be encouraged to record their practice, then listen to it and evaluate it.

Motivation

Pupils will practise only if they are motivated to do so. There are two principal types of motivation. *Extrinsic* motivation is influenced by factors such as examinations, parents, peers, concerts, teachers' feedback and praise. *Intrinsic* motivation is influenced by pupils' own feelings about their learning. To practise effectively, a combination of extrinsic and intrinsic motivation is desirable, particularly in the case of younger pupils. Parental support and encouragement are always important to a child but especially necessary in the early stages of learning, when aural, cognitive, musical, performance and technical skills all need to be developed.

The difficulty most teachers encounter is how best to encourage pupils to become intrinsically motivated. Primarily, teachers must always be enthusiastic in their teaching so that pupils enjoy playing in their lessons. As a result of teachers' modelling (and this includes all aspects of playing, including posture), pupils will be encouraged to play – and practise – at home. If, as a result of praise and encouragement from their teacher, pupils leave their lessons believing they can succeed, they will be more inclined to practise voluntarily. It is essential that pupils enjoy playing, and teachers need to offer pupils additional incentives from time to time in order to keep the level of motivation high (for example, by providing information about suitable ensembles, workshops and concerts that they might listen to or attend, and so on).

Beginners tend to become more motivated if they are asked to practise music which is predominantly fun to play but which also contains repetitive technical sections (the content of which pupils must have understood during the lesson). After the early stages of learning, pupils can become more involved in making decisions with their teacher about half-termly or termly learning objectives and the tasks and activities required to achieve them. Pupils' increased understanding of agreed practice targets will help to contribute to effective practice between lessons and will help to foster intrinsic motivation. The use of open and probing questions to assess knowledge and understanding can help encourage intrinsic motivation at all levels since pupils, even from a relatively young age, may consequently adopt a questioning approach to their practice at home.

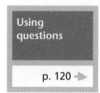

Using questions

p. 120 ➡

11

Lesson planning for groups

Leo Turner

Teachers who are used to dealing with individual pupils already have many of the instrumental and musical skills needed to teach groups. However, they will need a range of strategies to manage the behaviour and learning of several pupils together, and to deal with the fact that styles and rates of learning differ from pupil to pupil. This may appear daunting, but it is easily managed with a little forward thinking.

Group lessons have to be carefully planned and structured. Teachers must be pro-active, managing the direction and progress of the lesson, and having clear ideas about what they hope to achieve and the ability to share these with the group. Pro-active teachers discuss with the group targets for the term and for each lesson. They keep their eyes and ears open and use their observations to plan future lessons. They establish what they want the group to achieve and plan for it in the long, medium and short term. They consider the structure of each lesson and how to challenge the more able without discouraging the less able. Above all they plan both for the group and for its individual members.

> I generally find that teaching in groups requires particular preparation and planning. The teacher needs to be creative in finding ways of accommodating the different abilities found within most groups; e.g. extension activities for the more able. These could be rhythm variations for beginners or some kind of composition for more established players. KB

Different levels of planning

When planning group lessons, teachers need to consider what they hope to achieve in several different timescales: the long term (one year), the medium term (one school term or half-term) and the short term (a lesson). (Instead of measuring in units of time, some instrumental teachers may find it helpful to make long-term plans in terms of moving the group from one level of achievement to another – a grade or set of skills, for example.)

Note the use of the word 'achieve'. Plan what you want the group to *achieve*, not what you want it to do. The two approaches are different. Achievement calls for both *aim* and *activity*: the teacher plans to develop a specific area of technique or musicianship (the aim), and gathers the necessary musical material and activities (the activity). If the aim is not identified, the lesson is based solely on activity; this merely occupies the group rather than helping it to progress.

The **long-term plan** defines fundamental aims for the group. It considers what should be taught to the group and identifies areas for development. It should include listening skills, technical development, applying knowledge and encouraging pupils to evaluate their work. It will also include opportunities for group members to play individually and together, to create, to explore and to perform.

The long-term plan should build on previous experiences, featuring a broad, balanced range of musical activities. It should be flexible, accommodating work for more and less able pupils. To challenge pupils in different ways, various teaching and learning styles must be used. A long-term plan could include opportunities for the group to explore, create and develop musical ideas using different starting points (for example, ostinato, drones, poems or pictures).

The **medium-term plan** is created by dividing the long-term plan into manageable units which feature objectives for the term or half-term (for example, 'to develop dynamic range'; 'to improvise short melodic phrases on a pentatonic scale'; 'to devise rhythmic ostinatos'; 'to develop good practice routines'). The medium-term plan should also contain the musical material and activities you will use to achieve your objectives.

> The teacher should have a clear idea of where the group as a whole should have got to over a period of time. This medium-term planning and target setting should be discussed and agreed with the pupils as part of the lesson process. Usually some of this will be put into the practice diary so that they can understand where the week-to-week practice goals fit into the longer-term strategy.   RPr

Next, use the medium-term plan to create **short-term plans** for each lesson. These must be concise and manageable, because you need to allow the outcome of each lesson to feed directly into the objectives and activities for the next one. This is an important aspect of planning. Teachers deal with real pupils and situations, and have to be aware of pupils' needs from week to week and plan accordingly. Plan questions into the lesson; reinforce the answers with activities. Vary the teaching strategies too.

> Perhaps even more importantly than in individual lessons, short-, mid- and long-term planning needs to be effective and efficient. Teachers need to think as much about skill acquisition and knowledge building as about the pieces and exercises that get pupils to that point.
>
> MR

If this provokes daunting images of reams of paperwork, remember that plans can be reused in different situations. A long-term plan for the first year of group lessons could be used for all your first-year groups, with only a little fine-tuning for each context. The same could apply for the medium-term plan. While it may change slightly for each group, in essence it would have many of the same objectives and activities.

Creating your plans

The long-term plan must provide a broad range of technical, creative, appraising and listening skills. Each of these is then divided into medium- and short-term plans. For example, a long-term plan may contain the aim:

- Create rhythmical and melodic patterns using a limited range of notes.

In the medium-term plan this could become an objective:

- Create word rhythms using a question-and-answer structure.

An activity exploring this objective then becomes part of the short-term plan:

- Create short word rhythms based on food (for example 'fish and chips', 'beans on toast', 'sausage, egg and chips'). Clap these while saying the words, then without the words. Can some of the group tap a steady beat while the rest clap? Pupils perform these rhythms on their instruments.

Then, if you feel this activity worked well, you could feed the outcome into the next lesson plan:

- Revise word rhythms as last week. Use these with the notes E and G to create short melodic phrases. Can children repeat each word rhythm and melody four times? Can they teach their phrases to others?

Keep a brief record of activities and objectives. Look at where the pupils are and where they might be by the end of the session. Be realistic about what can be achieved in that time and be prepared for development and change. A group may respond differently from how you expected; the intuitive teacher will move the goalposts and change the plan for the next lesson. It is useful to keep a note of the repertoire being studied, effective exercises and games (what worked and what didn't), the vocal history of the pupil, information on other instruments they are learning, grades achieved, weak areas, strong areas, and so on. Encourage the pupils within the group to keep a diary of things to be practised and studied throughout the week. They might also like to write down how the practice went and report back any difficulties or triumphs in the next lesson.   HP

Delivering your plans

Think of a lesson in three phases – a beginning, a middle and an end. Share your aims at the beginning; develop ideas in the middle; and assess and reflect at the end. During each phase, monitor progress against the plan by asking yourself questions.

The **beginning** gets the children ready to play. It prepares pupils for learning and sets the scene for the rest of the lesson. Objectives and expected outcomes are shared at this point. For example: 'Today we are going to continue our work on ostinato and revise the work you have done on rhythms. I am also going to teach you a new note.'

The beginning should feature an activity or game that engages the whole group. If possible, link this to the main activity, and deliver it at a lively pace to get the pupils' musical brains in gear. For example:

Teacher: 'What's an ostinato?'
Group: 'A pattern that repeats itself.'
Repeat this question and answer several times to a pulse, generating a rhythm.
Teacher: 'Now let's play that word rhythm on our instruments.'

And in this way the lesson then moves forward into the main activity. Or, if the main piece is in G major, improvisations around the scale could be used, or call-and-response activities in G.

The key questions here are:

- Is the whole group musically engaged?
- Is the activity related to the main focus of the lesson?
- Is the pace suitable?
- Does the group understand the lesson objectives?

The **middle** contains the main focus of the plan, and is usually the longest part of the lesson. It may introduce a new technique, concept or piece, or consolidate previous work. As this part of the lesson unfolds the teacher needs to keep the lesson aims in mind and in the minds of the group, so that pupils remember why they are doing what they are doing. Features of this section should include:

- Demonstration by pupils or teacher. The teacher should provide examples of tone, phrasing, and so on. Pupils should also demonstrate to each other and discuss each other's playing. This helps you assess their understanding.
- The use of questions to reinforce learning and understanding. For example, if you began with the ostinato idea above, in the middle of the lesson you could ask pupils to explain the key features of an ostinato.
- The use of mistakes as teaching points. Create an environment where making a mistake is not a problem. Engage the group in discussing why something went wrong and how to correct it.
- Pupils working individually. If appropriate every pupil should make an individual contribution to the lesson.
- A range of activities demonstrating the same point. Can pupils write down rhythms as well as read them? Again, to develop the ostinato idea, some of the group could play an ostinato rhythm; others could try to clap it, describe it or write it down.
- Praise for success. Take good work for granted at your peril!

Think about concentration levels within the group: if the lesson gets stuck try another approach. Monitor whether the lesson is leading towards the objectives, and consider how to develop next week's lesson as a result.

Key questions here are:

- Are different teaching strategies used?
- Do pupils understand why they are doing the activity?
- Do pupils recognize improvement?
- Do I praise pupils if they improve?
- Does each individual contribute?
- Is the music suitable for a range of abilities?

The **end** reflects on what has been achieved. This is the most important part of the lesson, so leave time; much good work can be undone by rushing this. Make the group aware of what has improved, and how this happened. Reiterate the aims of the lesson, then share and celebrate the achievement:

> 'Today we played the notes E and G and we produced a clear tone. Well done, you worked really well.'

Then, use questions to reinforce specific points:

> 'What do we really have to think about when playing this new note?'
> 'Can anyone suggest why Mary's note sounded fuzzy at first?'
> 'What did Mary do to improve it?'
> 'What else do you think improved in the lesson?'
> 'How did we improve the middle section of the piece?'

Using questions

p. 120 →

Key questions for the teacher here are:

- Did we achieve what we set out to achieve?
- How, why and what are the group going to practise for next week?
- Did I question pupils about their achievement?
- Did I celebrate success?
- Did I finish on a positive note?

In conclusion

Group teaching has real advantages if well planned. Consider what you want your pupils to achieve and make long-, medium- and short-term plans for your aims. Vary teaching styles and materials. Be observant during lessons: use your observations to plan future lessons. Be flexible. Does your material challenge the more able without discouraging the less able? Consider the structure of the lesson and ask yourself questions as you work through it.

Effective planning helps you to teach better and your pupils to learn more successfully; but it is not a 'must do' list to follow regardless of what is happening around you. While

individual and group responses can to some extent be anticipated, they can never be predicted with absolute certainty. Not every situation and every response from each group member can be planned for. If what you have planned is not appropriate, change it. Good teachers will quickly realize if a lesson is not going to work and find a different short-term approach, while still directing the lesson towards well-planned long-term aims.

12

Assessment for groups

Leo Turner

All the time we are teaching we are assessing. We make judgements and decisions regarding how a lesson is developing and consider the best way forward. As we observe, we decide how to reinforce technical points or musical concepts. From pupils' responses, we set new targets. By assessing, we devise activities for future lessons and move towards the medium- and long-range learning objectives we have planned.

Usually, other more formal assessments will also be made of a group's work. These could include examinations, concerts and recordings, as well as formal assessment based on learning objectives.

The importance of assessment

Assessment affects motivation. Consider how pupils would learn if there were no assessment – no concerts, exams, recordings; no questions, lesson aims or feedback; no reports and no parents' evenings. This would substantially reduce motivation. Conversely, pupils can be equally demotivated if they feel that every note they play is being monitored. So assessment needs to be integral to the learning process; and at least part of it should be informal, delivered through games and activities.

Assessment not only motivates our work: it also affects how we work. Teachers and pupils work differently when assessment is expected. If we enter pupils for an examination, we have a clear idea of what will be examined, and aim to meet the assessment criteria. Because of this, we teach differently, and pupils will learn differently. And, from a teacher's point of view, asking for evidence of what has been learnt is an excellent way of assessing how well we have taught. Properly incorporated

...if they feel that every note they play is being monitored...

into teaching and learning, assessment becomes a real engine for development of pupils and teacher alike.

Different types of assessment

Group teachers assess pupils in a variety of ways, not just to monitor progress but to maintain motivation. Below are some of the main assessment strategies that group teachers need.

Formative assessment is the continual monitoring of progress and development. It is assessment for learning and should be made by the teacher and pupils during the lesson. In the light of the outcomes of the lesson, teacher and pupils decide what the group is going to learn next, so details such as what to practise for the next week (and why) will come from this type of assessment. Questions, feedback and engaging pupils in their own learning are key factors here.

Summative assessment is an assessment of learning – a snapshot of what has been learnt. It normally happens at the end of a unit of work or a piece being studied. Wherever possible, the group should be involved in this process – it should not only be the teacher giving marks out of 10. However, some forms of summative assessment are less suitable for this than others.

An examination is one example of summative assessment. Pupils work on pieces, scales, aural and sight-reading skills and are then assessed on how well they have performed. Another example is when a teacher considers how well a group has met medium-range learning objectives – at the end of term, for instance.

Making a recording of a group's performance at key moments in its development is a valuable form of summative assessment. It provides a permanent reference point to assess development over a period of time. Likewise the concert performance of a work learnt during term is a natural, exciting summative assessment.

Peer-group assessment and **self-assessment** are invaluable too. Developing pupils' awareness of their progress, and fostering their ability to remedy things that are not working, are fundamental to all teaching. For this to happen, pupils must be actively engaged in the assessment process. This self-examination should be encouraged at every point of assessment, be it formative or summative.

> A set of scales may be set to be tested a few weeks hence. Pupils will perform them individually, with everyone in the group giving an assessment. Criteria will be agreed beforehand – tempo, intonation, shifting, and so on. This encourages pupils to analyse both what they play and what they hear from their peers. This is a useful learning tool in group lessons. Too much formal assessment can be very cumbersome for the teacher if it involves recording lots of information on a regular basis; the danger is that it leads to too much assessment and not enough teaching.
>
> KB

Developing formative assessment strategies

We plan to assess: we assess to plan. The two activities are inextricably linked. When we plan lessons, we ask ourselves how we will engage the group in learning and how we intend to assess that learning. When we assess, we gather details of how the group and its individuals are progressing against our plans. Over time these details form a clear picture of pupils' development.

From the outset, therefore, we need to make clear our objectives and assessment criteria. These should be shared with the group so that pupils can be involved in the assessment process. Statements like 'Today we are going to...' and 'And at the end of the lesson we should be able to...' clarify aims for pupils. Write these on the board, or use handouts – many pupils respond better to a written statement.

Express the aims simply and clearly. For example:

Today we are going to:

- play loud and quiet sounds for different animals in 'Old Macdonald';
- play 'Conductor' and start and stop together;
- learn to play the note G.

Then, throughout the lesson and at the end, revisit these aims and consider whether they are being met. Use a range of strategies for this. For example, there are several different ways to assess how well group members have learnt to hold their instruments. Firstly, we can look and listen. Secondly, we can ask pupils what the key points or skills are. And thirdly, we can turn the assessment into an activity by asking pupils to stand up, turn around three times, pick up their instruments and assume a good posture. All of these will provide information about how well this skill has been learnt, and will suggest ways of developing it.

Using questions in formative assessment

Questions are an essential assessment tool. Asking questions reveals a great deal about pupils' understanding and how effectively we are teaching. Pupils' responses indicate the best way forward, or tell us if something needs clarification. In essence there are two types of question: open and closed.

Closed questions require limited responses. They can tell us if a pupil has learnt a fact, and are useful for establishing knowledge of specific details. For example, pupils need to know what *forte* means: we need to know that they know. Asking 'What does *forte* mean?' could lead to 'Are you actually playing louder?' Both these closed questions would help you assess pupils' knowledge of the concept of *forte*.

However, if we ask 'How many beats in a bar are there in this piece?' the response – though it may be correct – does not tell us how pupils know the answer. Did they look at the time signature, work it out aurally or simply guess? In this instance, pupils' responses to a closed question reveal little about their grasp of rhythm and pulse; we need a more sophisticated tool.

Open questions invite exploration and discussion. For example, the open question 'Why do we have time signatures?' reveals far more about pupils' understanding than the closed question above about beats in a bar. Likewise, questions such as 'How will you practise that passage this week?' or 'How could we improve our ensemble playing there?' engage the entire group and will promote demonstration by the pupils or teacher. Groups may need help getting used to this; if necessary, lead pupils towards answers by using further questions.

Open questions nurture self-assessment. Asking 'Where should your arm be?' or 'Describe what it feels like when your thumb is in the correct place' encourages pupils to reflect, consider and improve. Questions like this also encourage peer-group assessment: ask them of an individual and invite comment from other group members. For instance, if you ask an individual 'Can you show us how you hold your instrument?', you could follow it up with 'That's really good. There's just one thing I think you need to do. Can anyone make a suggestion?' A response from another group member – 'I think he needs to …' – could lead to a further open question like 'Can anyone tell me why we hold the instrument like this?'

Here are a few things to remember when asking questions:

- Wait for the answer! Let pupils think – if they are thinking, it is probably because you have asked a good question!
- Do not let pupils call out – have a behaviour code in place.
- Pupils should feel safe to get the answer wrong. (Open questions are good in this respect, because they do not always have 'right' and 'wrong' answers.) If answers provoke laughter, make sure the group laughs with the individual, never at them.
- Do not answer the question yourself. If pupils are having difficulty, ask other questions that will lead them to the answer.
- If an answer is incorrect, do not say so. There are learning opportunities for group pupils if you encourage them to discover why an individual has given a particular answer.

Assessing groups: assessing individuals

Assessment in a group context poses particular challenges. Teachers need to assess many areas of a group's progress; they also need to assess the development of both the group and individuals within it. One member of the group may excel at improvising while another feels more comfortable reading notation. Individuals should be given the opportunity to express themselves and their skills within the group.

Groups give teachers the opportunity to assess individuals' progress in different ways. For example, if you ask one pupil to demonstrate a technique to the others, you assess not only the individual's skill but also the ability of other group members as they consider and apply this knowledge. Groups also offer the resource of peer assessment, which can be a powerful tool if sensitively handled. For example, one pupil could watch the rest of the group play and comment on technique or musicianship. Often pupils accept and act upon constructive criticism from their peers more readily than that given by the teacher.

> Summative assessments will not be suitable for all pupils. It would be a mistake to enter everyone in a group lesson for an examination if it is not appropriate for them all. This can be problematic for group teachers as some children will be demotivated if most of their group take an examination and they do not. So it is very important to stress all other achievements too – playing in school assemblies and concerts or learning a particular piece really well. The teacher's own summative assessment could be a certificate for something particularly relevant to an individual child.   KB

The group is made up of individuals, and each pupil's progress will be different. The assessment criteria used in *A Common Approach 2002* are useful here:

- all pupils will…
- most pupils will…
- some children will have progressed further and will…

For example, consider assessing a group playing rounds. *All* children will be able to play the easier phrases. *Most* children will be able to play all the phrases. *Some* children will have progressed further and will be able to connect the phrases and play an independent part. So the group works together on the same piece but the assessment criteria are layered so that group members can succeed at different levels.

Or consider assessing a group's understanding of a structure like the twelve-bar blues. At the outset we may have the following expectations: *all* children will be able to play root notes with some guidance from the teacher; *most* children will internalize the structure and play root notes of the chords to a backing CD with no help from the teacher; *some* will internalize the structure and be able to play root notes and other notes from the chords without the teacher's help. At the end we can consider whether these expectations were met, and if not, why not.

> Assessment needs to ascertain the reasons for any particular progress (or lack of it). The interesting part of this process is that if a teacher reflects on an individual pupil's challenges and evolves strategies to help, these may well assist in the development of the whole class.   MR

Development and achievement can be recorded in many ways, but it is best to avoid openly giving marks and grades. Your feedback on how to develop is far more important. One way to record assessment is to mark the register in three colours:

- green: understanding;
- yellow: is getting there;
- red: needs some consolidation.

This information then leads into more formal report writing and feedback.

Assessing is positive and moves us forward. But in a group there is the danger of comparing pupils with each other rather than assessing them as individuals. Comparing pupils lowers the self-esteem of the less able, and may demotivate the more able.

13

Feedback and reporting

In conclusion

Assessment gives real insight into how pupils are learning, and clear indications of what they should be learning. Skilful group teachers use carefully balanced methods of assessment that consider the progress of both the group and its individuals. Assessment is a vital, planned part of each lesson. The group should be actively engaged in every level of the process; this will enable pupils to become independent learners and individual musicians.

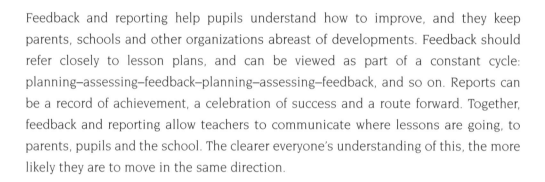

Feedback and reporting for group teachers

Leo Turner

Feedback and reporting help pupils understand how to improve, and they keep parents, schools and other organizations abreast of developments. Feedback should refer closely to lesson plans, and can be viewed as part of a constant cycle: planning–assessing–feedback–planning–assessing–feedback, and so on. Reports can be a record of achievement, a celebration of success and a route forward. Together, feedback and reporting allow teachers to communicate where lessons are going, to parents, pupils and the school. The clearer everyone's understanding of this, the more likely they are to move in the same direction.

Feedback in a group context

Feedback should help pupils to develop. It should focus on the quality of their playing and not on comparisons between pupils. Give feedback as pupils get to grips with a technical issue or a new concept. Emphasizing the positive and highlighting the group's progress is a powerful motivator, building confidence and self-esteem. 'Well done; that was much better. Now how can we make sure we finish together?' is much better than 'That was a complete mess at the end. Do it again after four.' It is particularly crucial to end every lesson on a positive note.

As well as giving positive feedback to the group, remember that the group consists of individuals. If one individual has found a particular technique difficult and has now mastered it, celebrate this: 'You have worked really hard on that and it has paid off. Well done.' Be sensitive to the impact of negative comments, and try not to single out individuals. 'We didn't do that very well, did we?' would have a negative effect; even worse would be 'You didn't do that very well.'

Rewards like stickers and stars can work well in a group situation but should be handled carefully. One-to-one lessons are private and such rewards generally present few problems, but in a group there is a risk that pupils will think they are being compared. Comparison damages the motivation and self-esteem of less able pupils. It may also have a negative effect on the more able, who, if rewarded every week, may question the need to keep trying.

If you do give rewards, make them reflect the quality, not the quantity, of pupils' work. One idea is to give individuals a raffle ticket for each piece of positive work or behaviour, and at the end of each half-term draw a ticket to win a small prize. (Check that the school or institution is happy with this procedure first, and select a prize that meets with its approval.) This way everybody is motivated and has a chance of winning.

Report writing for groups

Most schools and educational institutions will at some point expect a written report on the pupils you teach. This is usually every term or every year. Many of them will have their own system in place regarding the style and frequency of reporting. If you teach privately you may have designed your own report form and have more control over this.

Although you have been teaching pupils as a group, parents will expect a report on their child as an individual. Group members will have been working towards the same goals but each individual will have different strengths and weaknesses. For example, one may have excelled at creative music-making but have poor posture. Be aware of these differences when writing reports.

> I always consider the individual first and foremost. Their contribution to the group is commented upon. A class teacher gives a report on the child not the class. How the child responds in the class is relevant but not the main comment. I find I do the same.
>
> RPe

During the weeks leading up to your report writing, gather information about the group and individuals – the more you gather, the more informative your reports will be. Begin by referring to your lesson plans. The long-term plan will show the big picture, enabling you to see how much progress has been made towards each objective. Medium-term plans will identify more specific areas, while short-term plans tend to give better insight into how individuals have been working. Make brief notes on each group member, flagging up areas that you wish to comment on. By definition, group teachers have a lot of pupils – these notes will really help when you are on report number 178 with a hundred to go! Consider the following when report writing:

11

Lesson planning for groups

Start positively

Bring the pupil's achievement to the fore: 'James can play, read and improvise short tunes and phrases on the first three strings with increasing control.'

Highlight areas for development

Suggest how the pupil could improve in these areas, in a way that is meaningful to the reader. For example, the comment 'needs to improve posture' may mean little to the parent or pupil. 'Needs to improve posture by sitting on the edge of the chair when playing' is much more informative.

Avoid stating the obvious

'Should practise more' applies to most pupils; a remark like 'Needs to consolidate the work covered in lessons with 10 minutes' practice each day' gives a better idea of how to practise.

Do not try to cover too much

Focus on the key areas you have been working on and make your comments relevant to these.

Do not focus solely on achievement

Think about progress too. A pupil may have been really struggling with a particular technique and is now making real progress with it. This needs comment and praise.

Focus on comments, not grades

Many report forms have grade boxes and a comments section. The two should reflect each other. Parents and pupils tend to focus on the grade because it is easy to measure. But while B+ is a clear mark, it says nothing about how or what the pupil needs to improve – so make your comments as informative as possible.

Involve the group

Before you write your reports ask how pupils think they have progressed. What pieces of music did they enjoy playing? What can they do now that they could not do last term? How did they achieve this? What do they think they need to do next? It is important that pupils have this input and take ownership of their reports.

Your reports reflect your teaching

If you find yourself writing 'Has difficulty maintaining steady rhythm' on every report, ask yourself if you have chosen appropriate material or teaching styles for your group. If reference to a particular technique keeps appearing on your reports, you may need to teach it differently.

> It is important to write a report at the end of a session of work. The report is for the pupil so that they can see what has been achieved and areas of improvement. If possible always discuss these issues with the pupil so that they can give their opinion from their side. It is amazing what you discover when you talk to a pupil! The report is also useful for parents as they can see what the pupil has been or should have been doing throughout the session.
>
> HP

Make three copies of your reports. Keep one set for your own files. This will help you monitor pupils' progress over a period of time. (When writing reports, refer back to earlier ones. This will help you see not only how pupils have developed but also how your teaching is developing.) Give one set to the school or organizing body, and give a copy of each individual's report to the parent or guardian, by post or via the pupil. You might enclose an invitation to attend a parents' evening to discuss the report. (If you work in a school, there will probably be procedures in place for reporting and feedback. Before you begin reporting, establish whether you are expected to follow these.)

Giving feedback to parents of group pupils

Group teaching usually takes place in a school or educational institution, and parents are not normally present. So your written reports – and pupils' progress in general – may need to be discussed with the parents. This may be at a formal parents' evening, or during a more casual talk with the parent, say at the end of the lesson (you should arrange a mutually convenient time and place).

Having arranged the meeting, have all the relevant information to hand. Think about what you want to say, but listen carefully to the parents as well. (You may want to take notes of issues they raise.) Set a time limit on the meeting beforehand with the parents and try to stick to this without being rude. Here are a few tips about this sort of meeting:

- Be positive at the start. 'Thank you for coming to discuss John's progress.' This instantly implies that progress has been made.
- Mirror the written report. Concentrate on your comments, not the grades. Discuss what pupils have learnt, the progress they have made, and how you plan to move forward.
- Share your aims for the term or year. This way you can be specific about this year's achievement and what you plan to achieve in the future.
- Turn off your mobile phone. It will ring if you do not!

Many parents will ask how to help their children practise at home. Even if they have no musical background, they can still help. Encouraging effective practice routines (little and often) and praising good work are vital to a child's development. Simple things like keeping the instrument handy and available will help. (Keeping the instrument on top of a wardrobe in the loft makes practising an effort!) Encouraging group members to practise together, listen to music and go to concerts will all help pupils' musical development.

If parents do not feel their child has made sufficient progress and you disagree, remain calm but firm. Emphasize the quality and variety of playing opportunities you give the group, as well as the qualities of the individual in question. If parents are pushing for the child to take an examination and you feel this is inappropriate, do not be forced into a situation with which you are unhappy. However, it is vital not to respond in a negative way or get personal.

Some parents may see a meeting like this as an opportunity to raise problems or issues they have with the school or class teacher. If this happens, suggest they contact the school head. Once again, remain calm and stick to the issues relating to the musical development of the pupil.

> Group teaching presents the opportunity for feedback to be the norm. Liaising with parents is as important as in one-to-one teaching, but the teacher needs to be clear about the boundaries here. It would be easy for a parent (or an adult in an adult class) to demand more individual attention than is reasonable – this could be problematic if done at an inappropriate time or place.   MR

Giving feedback to schools

Visiting teachers need to become part of the school's musical life. To do this effectively, it is vital to establish good methods of communication. Class teachers will not always be available for discussion when you are in school, so try the following approaches.

Sign in on arrival

If the school does not have a book for visiting teachers, suggest they get one. This will prevent any possible conflict and reinforce your register. You (and staff members) might also leave messages in this book regarding any problems or questions you may have. This will also alert the school to any particular difficulties, for example if a pupil regularly fails to attend lessons (and if you are teaching a group you cannot leave to search for an individual).

Allow time for feedback

Arrange a time to talk to the member of staff responsible for your work. This may be only once a term, but it is important. Discuss what your groups are working on, how individuals are doing, and any planned concerts. Give notification if you intend to reorganize any groups. Also, find out what the focus of classroom music will be for each year group: if year 5 is working on rounds for a term, you might plan this into some of your lessons.

You may also wish to discuss your reports. It is a good idea to give copies of reports to the staff member before you give them to the parents. If parents have problems, they are likely to contact the school rather than the group teacher, so provide staff with the necessary information.

In conclusion

Planning, assessing and feedback are interlinked. We can give effective feedback only if pupils are clear about lesson aims and how their work will be assessed. Feedback should help pupils to make their own decisions and develop as individual musicians. Feedback to parents not only informs them of their child's progress but also empowers them to help their child to develop.

Report writing should provide a clear snapshot of pupils' achievements and plans for future work. Although it is seen as a comment on the pupil's progress, it also reflects your own teaching methods.

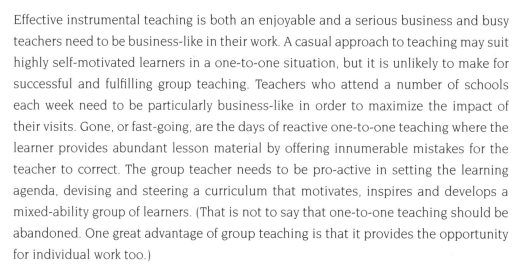

14

Business aspects of group teaching

Richard Crozier

Effective instrumental teaching is both an enjoyable and a serious business and busy teachers need to be business-like in their work. A casual approach to teaching may suit highly self-motivated learners in a one-to-one situation, but it is unlikely to make for successful and fulfilling group teaching. Teachers who attend a number of schools each week need to be particularly business-like in order to maximize the impact of their visits. Gone, or fast-going, are the days of reactive one-to-one teaching where the learner provides abundant lesson material by offering innumerable mistakes for the teacher to correct. The group teacher needs to be pro-active in setting the learning agenda, devising and steering a curriculum that motivates, inspires and develops a mixed-ability group of learners. (That is not to say that one-to-one teaching should be abandoned. One great advantage of group teaching is that it provides the opportunity for individual work too.)

This chapter looks at some of the practical and business aspects of teaching groups of children either at home or in a school. Some of the topics are explored further in other chapters of the book, so it is worth following the links at the side of the page if you wish to pursue something in more detail.

Time management

With a prescribed number of minutes' teaching available at a given school, and limited travelling time before work commences at the next one, teachers need to be punctual and organized. Effective time management is as much a state of mind as an exercise in clock-watching. It necessitates assessing the amount of time needed to do something as much as planning the lesson activities themselves, and it requires teachers to judge carefully the amount of time that will be spent actually making music as distinct from talking about it. Teachers who practise good time management must not only lead by example but must also do everything possible to encourage their pupils to develop the same time-management skills. For example, pupils need to be made aware that being punctual for the start of the lesson does not only mean reaching the room on time: it means being there in sufficient time to prepare the instrument, get the music out, tune up, and so on, so that valuable teaching time is not spent on these things.

Planning

It may be impossible for most teachers to make detailed lesson plans for all of their groups, but it is essential to plan and develop the range of strategies to be used and to consider the materials needed for teaching each group. Thought should also be given to the amount of time spent in each lesson on activities that will develop sight-reading, technique, improvisation, transposition, phrasing, and so on. Such planning could be supported by one of the instrumental curriculum documents currently available, such as *A Common Approach 2002*, and will benefit, too, from being linked to the classroom activities children are likely to be undertaking (these are detailed in the National Curriculum and its associated Schemes of Work). Teachers planning group work also need to give thought to the issues of progress, achievement and attainment and the assessment of these. 'Progress' refers to pupils' improvement in any of a large number of areas including breathing, posture, reading notation, tone production, and so on. 'Achievement' normally refers to the accomplishments of an individual, whereas 'attainment' may be measured through a summative assessment, for example an examination or a performance at a given point of a piece against fixed, perhaps national or international criteria.

11

Lesson planning for groups

12

Assessment for groups

Accountability

The effectiveness of teaching is measured through a range of accountabilities. For group teachers, accountability will come not only through pupils' examination results, festival performances, concerts, and so on but will also be measured through pupil and teacher attendance. Group teachers must therefore adopt or develop effective procedures to monitor attendance as well as assess and record progress, which enable reliable reporting to pupil, parent and school. Another facet of record-keeping, often overlooked by music teachers, is the business of tuition fees and payments for additional things such as reeds, strings, valve oil, cleaners, music, recordings and other miscellaneous items. Inexperienced teachers will soon be out of pocket unless they keep a careful record of what they have supplied to pupils. At the outset, find out

13

Feedback and reporting

...Inexperienced teachers will soon be out of pocket...

from the school whether learners will be expected to equip themselves with these items, or whether they are to be supplied by the visiting teacher or directly by the school. Then make the situation clear to pupils and their parents, informing them of the charges they are likely to encounter, and when and to whom payment is to be made.

> I produce a document circulated to schools giving package suggestions as regards to cost. Group lessons reduce the cost considerably to parents, so enabling more students to have lessons. This alone is a powerful reason for making group lessons available. However, the document continues by pointing out other advantages of group learning – that students learn from each other and quickly develop ensemble skills; that most of the instruments studied are used mainly in ensembles and developing sensitivity to each other is a vital part of any musician's training; and that it can also help GCSE students, as they have to produce an ensemble performance. RPe

Teaching environment

15

Links with schools

The immediate teaching environment is often outside the control of visiting teachers, but wherever possible try to ensure that the working space provided for the lesson – be it practice room, school hall, staff room or music room – is conducive to learning. It may be necessary to spend a few minutes tidying the room first – although in primary schools, where it is often the staff room that is used for group teaching, this may be diplomatically difficult! As starting points for creating a positive atmosphere for teaching and learning, an ideal teaching space might include: chairs; music stands; a piano or electronic keyboard; access to unpitched percussion instruments; a CD player; a MIDI-file player; a computer with relevant software; a mirror; water; good lighting; enough space to move around comfortably; and a sympathetic acoustic environment. Access to daylight and fresh air, coupled with appropriately restful decoration would complement this to good effect. This may be no more than a wish list, but it is essential for business-like visiting teachers to have a clear idea of what constitutes an effective teaching and learning space and to work towards this ideal. (You may wish to share this list with new clients at the start of a contract – though once again, this may require some diplomacy and courage.)

> Group teaching requires more space, naturally, than one-to-one. Traditional practice rooms (designed for individual piano lessons) are not big enough for individual trombone or cello lessons, let alone groups. Thus negotiation and a good relationship with schools are vital. All teachers should be prepared to move equipment around in the rooms in which they teach in order to ensure that the space available is at its most suitable.   RPr

Professional development

Once the academic year has begun, most teachers have little time for thought or reflection. For some visiting teachers, work can be a professionally lonely and isolated business, so it is important to take every opportunity to meet other teachers in similar circumstances, to keep skills as up to date as possible and to stay abreast of any administrative or policy changes on the part of the employer. To this end, Music Services are likely to provide regular staff meetings and (usually termly) In-Service Training (INSET) or Continuing Professional Development (CPD) days. For practical reasons, these are often timed for the beginning or end of term, neither of which is always ideal for professional refreshment, but they do play a vital role and you should make every effort to attend. Membership of a professional body may also provide the opportunity to meet colleagues working for other employers, or engaged in other branches of the music-teaching profession; some of these organizations will also provide help and advice – even legal support in the unlikely event that it becomes necessary. Within the employment structures offered by Music Services, opportunities for career advancement are often quite limited and it is therefore vital that teachers who want to make progress should take every opportunity to keep fully up to date with both the musical and educational aspects of their work.

Child protection

All adults who work with children need to be aware of child protection. As an employer the Music Service has certain statutory obligations to fulfil but, at a practical level, teachers need to be aware of the many issues involved when working with children. Here are some to bear in mind.

Instrumental lessons often take place in small rooms that may be away from the school's main teaching areas. When working in a small practice room it is essential to establish personal space for teachers and learners alike, for example by placing an empty chair between teacher and pupil, or by ensuring that members of the group regularly change places to avoid the same learner always being placed next to the teacher. If the door is not glazed, it should be left open if possible.

When teaching it is often easiest to reinforce a point by touching a finger or arm, but permission should always be sought from the learner before this is done rather than letting it become part of the routine.

Group teachers should also consider their place in the teaching group itself. Will you teach as a member of the group or stand facing the learners? Although space or the lack of it may be a deciding factor, it is also important to consider whether to address pupils face to face, or predominantly from one side or another. Each pupil learns best in a different way – some prefer the teacher on their left, others the right; some respond best when the teacher is in front, others behind. This is another reason to change the dynamic within the group by frequently changing places for learning and teaching. It also helps to overcome any notion of favouritism.

9

Psychology of group teaching

The instrumental or singing teacher can easily develop a relationship with pupils that is quite different from the one developed by class teachers. The small-group environment may easily lead to more personal conversations and it is vital that teachers maintain sufficient emotional distance from pupils in order to sustain an effective teacher–pupil dynamic. Over-familiarity of any kind is likely to lead in the long term to difficulties, so practise careful relationship management from the outset, making it clear to pupils what is acceptable and unacceptable.

In a number of places in this book, contributors suggest the use of video recording (to help pupils monitor their progress, to document their performances, or to use as part of examination submissions). If you intend to use video equipment, it is vital that you ask permission from the school, the parents and the pupils themselves, and that everyone is in agreement that recording should take place. (Some schools may well have their own routines in place for this sort of activity, so seek advice from the school administration.)

Group teaching at home

Teachers who work independently at home are also turning to group teaching both as an effective way of providing children with the best possible learning experience and as a way of maximizing their earning power. Again, the key factors, given that the teaching environment is suitably spacious, are the issues of preparation and time-keeping. Parents who bring children to lessons need to know how long the lesson will be; more than 5 minutes discrepancy may cause noticeable disruption to domestic schedules. Careful planning is essential to ensure that all the learners in the group are gainfully occupied throughout the session and that each individual goes away feeling that his or her individual needs have been addressed, be it overcoming a particular difficulty, starting a new piece, preparing for an exam, or going home to do some practice.

Beyond the lesson

Much of this book concentrates properly on what happens inside the teaching room, within the lesson. For most children this period of instrumental learning constitutes no more than 25 minutes of their entire school week, perhaps less than 2 per cent of their time spent in school. The exhortation 'Don't forget to do some practice' rings in the ears of teachers, but may go in one ear and out the other for most pupils. Teaching what, when and how to practise are key elements in teachers' work if they are to achieve sustained success and long-term progression with learners. Planning this part of teaching is just as important as lesson planning, and needs just as many strategies. Pupils who learn together in groups can be encouraged to practise in groups and continue helping one another to overcome difficulties, just as they are enabled to do in their lessons.

10

Practice

15

Links with schools

Richard Crozier

Most group teaching is undertaken by instrumental teachers who visit schools, but in any event, the vast majority of pupils learning instruments in groups will be in full-time education. The work of peripatetic teachers will be effective only if they develop a broad understanding of the work of their classroom colleagues, the administrative requirements of the individual school, the school music curriculum, and the school's particular aims and ethos. The need for visiting instrumental teachers to develop effective links with schools is paramount. It is therefore important that they understand how music works in school.

Music in schools

Maintained schools in the United Kingdom apply their own country's statutory classroom music curriculum (in England, Wales and Northern Ireland) or guidelines (in Scotland); this provision is complemented and strengthened by instrumental tuition for a selected few. In England, the statutory classroom curriculum is set out across the four Key Stages that, since their introduction as part of the Education Reform Act (1988), have become the framework for all age-related school planning. Across the UK, music is compulsory for all children in Key Stages 1 to 3 (ages 5–14), and optional at Key Stage 4 (ages 14–16). Music in the classroom is focused on performing, composing and responding through listening and appraising. The English National Curriculum music document, for example, sets out what children should be taught and what they may be expected to achieve. It can be downloaded from the National Curriculum website (http://www.nc.uk.net). Schemes of Work to help teachers with their planning are published by the Department for Education and Skills (DfES; http://www.standards.dfes.gov.uk); these can also be accessed from the Qualifications and Curriculum Authority (QCA) website (http://www.qca.org.uk). Curricula differ in Wales, Scotland and Northern Ireland; details are available by following links on the National Curriculum site.

Whereas class music lessons are part of the statutory curriculum, instrumental tuition has always been seen as an extra-curricular activity. On average, no more than 10 per cent of the maintained school population has instrumental tuition; and this arguably disappointing figure actually represents a growth since the early 1990s. Starting to learn an instrument is not tied to any particular age-range, although it is widely accepted that to develop advanced skills on piano, or stringed instruments such as violin, it is better to start at an early age, say 5 or 6, whereas learning a woodwind instrument can begin later, at say 10 or 11, and still produce excellent results.

The role of the classroom music teacher

In the primary school, there are now far fewer teachers than there were with the necessary subject-specific skills and knowledge to deliver effectively a music curriculum for all. Though these specialists do still exist, music is more often taught by a non-specialist whose experience of music teaching and music-making may be very limited. However, it is often the case that among primary teachers a shortfall of musical expertise is compensated for by a better understanding of the issues associated with teaching and learning. There are a number of well-written music schemes available for the primary teacher that ensure good coverage of all of the National Curriculum's requirements. But no matter how good the scheme may be, nothing can overcome the fear experienced by a teacher trying to lead a boisterous class of 11-year-olds in a lesson where singing is required. In most secondary schools the principal music teacher is a trained music specialist with good subject-specific knowledge. By necessity, the main concern of these teachers will be delivering the curriculum to the larger group of potential learners that fall outside the 10 per cent having instrumental tuition.

It is a commonly held view in schools that children need to show aptitude for music in order for it to be considered appropriate for them to have instrumental lessons. A selection procedure, often based on an aural test, continues to be an accepted way of choosing pupils for instrumental tuition. For the school, there are some advantages to this. Firstly, it keeps the number of learners to a minimum when human and material resources are scarce. Secondly, it creates a special role for visiting instrumental teachers in that they can be reasonably certain of working with largely well-motivated pupils. (This is in sharp contrast with the work of classroom teachers, who have to take on all-comers.) It is this selection procedure that has, in part, enabled instrumental tuition to achieve the high standards that it has – but it has also caused it to be condemned as elitist. But surely the answer to this criticism is to make instrumental learning available to a larger proportion of the school population: plainly the children who find the selection test difficult are the very ones who are most in need of some informed musical tuition. (The UK government's 'Wider Opportunities' initiative is intended in part to address this issue. During 2003 a small number of music education organizations, in collaboration with the Department for Education and Skills, ran pilot schemes to offer more primary pupils the chance to take part in a greater range of musical experiences. As of spring 2004, the results of these pilots are under evaluation.)

The visiting instrumental teacher in school

Finding a suitable room is a common complaint. It helps if your timetable is clearly displayed and it pays to outline why you need a room with a piano, etc. If necessary, a line manager may be able to support you by putting something in writing. Timetabling is an issue in many schools and parents and students can become anxious about missing numeracy and literacy hours. If at all possible, and you have sufficient numbers in a school, it is advisable to rotate the timetable so the same class lesson is not missed every week. This is easier in secondary schools as junior school children tend not to be able to cope with different lesson times every week. Communication is the key and it is always best to ask.   KB

The visiting instrumental teacher is the ambassador for both the instrument(s) they teach and for instrumental learning itself. By forging good relationships with the secondary music department and the school, or in primary schools with the music co-ordinator and the head teacher, the instrumental teacher is in a position to influence key decisions about music in the school. Most visiting instrumental teachers find that pupils make the most progress when their host school has a thriving musical life of its own.

7

Using music technology

It can be useful to establish what children are learning in class and integrate this to some extent with group instrumental work. For example, working with small groups of pupils makes instrumental lessons ideal for including computer technology to support the learning. Pupils could use software to help them improve their aural skills, record their performances of pieces, create their own compositions, make simple arrangements to play in the lesson, and so on. With even a brief study of the music department's schemes of work, it should be easy to identify scope for further collaboration between the classroom curriculum and the instrumental curriculum. For instance, a study of blues (a common favourite in Key Stage 3) provides an ideal opportunity for the group teacher to explore chords, voicings, harmony and improvisation. Moving away from the tutor book or examination pieces to engage with this sort of creative work adds understanding to the learners' skill base, and encourages progress in aspects which are so often overlooked in instrumental learning.

> When working in schools it is useful to know about specific classroom music projects, areas of study, termly themes, and so on. Classroom teachers may, however, be too busy teaching to have detailed discussions with peripatetic instrumental teachers during their weekly visits to school. Where possible I encourage school music co-ordinators to supply me with any information they feel will help me fit my work into the school's music programme. I stress that by this I mean not only the concert programme and opportunities to play in assemblies but also the class teaching programme, and any ideas they have for ways in which my students could contribute to their class music lessons.
>
> AE

In a primary school it may be more appropriate for a visiting instrumental teacher to support a non-specialist classroom teacher by helping to deliver pre-instrumental classes, engaging children in rudimentary musical activities and raising their awareness of the possibilities of learning an instrument. Helping children to develop vital musical skills, albeit at a basic level, is just as important as starting to play the instrument itself, because when they do start on an instrument their progress will be more assured.

> With primary children, finding out what their topic is can help make links between class and instrumental lessons. A historical topic such as the Tudors provides good opportunities to find suitable repertoire. I recently had a year 6 group give a concert and presentation to a year 1 class who were doing 'sound' as their topic. The year 6 group enjoyed putting together their own programme and demonstrating how sound is produced on string instruments. This led to all the other instrumental teachers and their pupils doing 'a slot' with this class who had a rolling series of mini concerts covering all the instrumental specialisms.
>
> KB

Primary, middle and secondary schools may be the principal areas of employment for the group instrumental teacher but the many other categories of school should not be overlooked. Nursery schools, reception classes and other types of under-fives provision are ripe for musical development, and the instrumental teacher is ideally placed to lead and advise on musical activities which, in time, will stimulate interest in instrumental and singing tuition. Special schools catering specifically for children with emotional or behavioural difficulties, or physical special needs, are also places where children will benefit enormously from musical stimulation. In all of these schools the focus will be on developing basic musical skills, which in turn may lead to study on a specific instrument – putting music first rather than the instrument itself. It is this focus that is the hallmark of most successful instrumental teaching.

The growth of these relationships between classroom and instrumental teaching will also help to mitigate against children giving up as soon as they encounter difficulties. Once the instrumental learning process has begun, other motivational factors come into play. Experience has shown that children need lots of encouragement with learning in any subject area and music is no exception. Alongside this encouragement comes the diagnostic assessment which is at the heart of the teacher's work. A publicly recognized and formal summative assessment such as Music Medals complements the motivational links with school and home which may make the difference between an early departure from learning and the passage to lifelong learning – every teacher's ultimate goal for their pupils.

Other duties for the visiting instrumental teacher

While instrumental teachers may well have their own view of their mission in the school, or may be working to deliver an employer's mission statement, it is equally important to remember that, in all probability, the school will have its own interpretation of the purpose of instrumental teaching. In the secondary school, for example, the head of music may see it as the visiting instrumental teacher's job to create and run ensembles and, in some cases, the instrumental teacher may be brought in specifically to fulfil this purpose. This can be hugely rewarding for teachers and pupils alike – playing in an ensemble, at no matter how basic a level, will enable learners to develop important musical skills more easily than in isolated instrumental lessons. For some children, attending an ensemble will be the highlight of their school

16

Music Medals

Opportunities for performance

◀ p. 53

...the school will have its own interpretation of the purpose of instrumental teaching...

week. (For others it will provide an interesting diversion from the general school routine and for some it will be a chore.)

> The attitude of each school is very important and can range from the indifferent to: 'Can they play in assembly every week?' Children are very good at picking up signals: if a head teacher takes an interest then the children do feel that learning an instrument is of value.   KB

But ensemble work can also have its frustrations: among many other things, instrumental teachers need to consider how many ensembles they can cope with on a regular basis; where the music will be stored in the school; the budget for purchase of music for that ensemble; and the number of concerts they may be expected to attend. In some schools the work of the instrumental teacher has become completely subservient to the needs of the school orchestra, band or whatever ensemble is currently being developed. While this focus for activity has certain benefits, it may devalue the purpose of instrumental learning.

Curriculum support for the instrumental teacher

Many instrumental teachers working for a Local Education Authority (or similarly structured and funded Music Services) now find that they may be required to provide 'classroom support'. This will necessitate a thorough knowledge of the National Curriculum's requirements (see above for the website addresses).

It also serves to remind us that while a curriculum for classroom music teaching is a comparatively new requirement, the idea of a curriculum for instrumental and singing teachers is even newer. From the mid 1990s the Federation of Music Services (FMS) and the National Association of Music Educators (NAME) have worked together, latterly in association with the Royal College of Music, to produce an instrumental and vocal curriculum, *A Common Approach* (*ACA*, later revised as *A Common Approach 2002*). This sets out a curriculum for instrumental and vocal tuition supported by exemplar schemes of work as an aid to planning. Although *ACA* is non-statutory it has been widely adopted by Music Services. Its presence, leave alone its implementation, has already helped to raise awareness among instrumental teachers of the importance of planning, particularly where group teaching is involved. The document also makes links between instrumental lessons and the National Curriculum for classroom music, drawing attention to the importance and relevance in instrumental lessons of information and computer technology (ICT), composition, improvisation and music from other cultures.

16

Music Medals: an assessment syllabus for groups

Nigel Scaife

This chapter looks at how Music Medals (the Associated Board's assessments for group-taught pupils) reflect the special dynamics of group teaching, serve as a useful and versatile tool for group teachers, and provide a series of milestones to motivate and reward group learners on their musical journey. It sets out the aims of the syllabus, charts its development, and provides something of its philosophy and rationale.

It should be stressed that Music Medals form an assessment scheme and not an instrumental curriculum such as that outlined by *A Common Approach 2002*. Music Medals use a simple structure to assess the core activities of group learning: playing with others, playing solo and developing musicianship. The teacher ('Teacher-Assessor') makes the assessment during normal lesson time, then sends a video of the pupil taking his or her Medal to the Associated Board for moderation. While the assessments take place in groups, only one member of the group is actually assessed per Medal, so it is that particular individual, rather than the group, whose attainment is rewarded.

Music Medals embrace modern teaching approaches and technology in resourceful and innovative ways. Internet and scanning technology make the reporting and moderation of pupils' strengths and weaknesses an efficient, user-friendly process. All Teacher-Assessors are trained against exemplar performances and the fact that Medals are video recorded helps to ensure a high level of quality assurance.

Aims

The core aim in developing the syllabus was to find an assessment model that would fit comfortably with, and promote, good practice in group teaching. It was felt that

Music Medals should form a series of music assessments and not *instrumental* assessments; the focus is on the musical outcomes themselves, rather than the technical means of achieving them. In this way the assessments should not encroach on the teacher's remit by endorsing any given teaching style or philosophy. We wanted a syllabus model that would allow teachers to enter pupils for assessment without having to alter their lesson activities or approaches.

So the challenge was to match as closely as possible the content of the assessment to the activities of the group lesson – and to make its delivery easily manageable with minimal disruption to the teaching and learning process. With the length of group lessons being typically just 20 or 30 minutes, we felt it important to keep the administrative demands of assessment to an absolute minimum. The aim was to create a simple framework, with limited paperwork, that does not encroach too much on valuable teaching time. The model had to be flexible enough to accommodate the diverse range of both the size and constituency of groups themselves, and of the various approaches adopted in tutor and method books.

The concept of Medals (Copper, Bronze, Silver, Gold and Platinum) combines the need to reward pupils from the earliest stages of learning (in a way that they will find motivational and worthwhile) with a step-by-step scheme that is distinctive from graded exams and easily understood. Whereas typically it might take over two years for a beginner to reach Grade 1 level, the Copper Medal is designed for pupils who have been learning for less than a year. Accepting that pupils start at different ages and learn at different rates, each subsequent Medal is designed to form a potentially annual target. The Platinum Medal is placed within the National Qualifications Framework at Intermediate Level, the same level as GCSE.

Music Medal	UK National Qualifications Framework
Copper	Entry Level
Bronze	Foundation Level
Silver	Foundation Level
Gold	Foundation Level
Platinum	Intermediate Level

Another core aim was to accommodate mixed-ability groups and to allow the achievements of weaker pupils to be recognized. Many group teachers have found it difficult to find materials that cater for the range of abilities within their groups. While a few tutor and method books contain useful duets, trios and quartets with differentiated parts, often there are not enough examples to meet the needs of pupils, and many teachers have to spend valuable time writing their own arrangements. To support the Music Medals assessments, it was clearly necessary to provide a set of flexible ensemble materials, specifically commissioned for group teaching, that would appeal to young learners and fill this crucial gap in resources. For each Medal and instrument there is a separate book of pieces. Each book contains pieces that combine individual parts at different ability levels. In this way, teachers can use the publications as an ongoing part of their teaching, allowing the assessment to become a natural part of the teaching and learning process. Some pupils will be working from the same tutor book for two or three years, so introducing a Music Medals book into the programme can be a refreshing change. Indeed, the motivational aspects of 'finishing the Medal book' and getting a new book of pieces can be significant for young learners, offering a valuable boost to confidence and morale.

The assessments also needed to be deliverable at a cost that is attractive to parents, and to have additional benefits for Music Services in terms of their monitoring procedures. Two areas have had an important bearing on cost: the structure of the Music Medals syllabus itself, and the use of technology both in the video recording of the assessments and in the online administration system.

Development

During the development phase many structures, mark schemes, modes of assessment and ways of recognizing the range of pupils' musical achievements were tried out. Different kinds of pupil profiling and combinations of 'internal' and 'external' assessment were considered in depth. However, differentiation and benchmarking were problematic, as two basic truths had to be acknowledged. Firstly, not all pupils have access to the same learning and performance opportunities; secondly, while judging effort and achievement are vital in formative assessment, providing the basis of termly reports, they cannot realistically form part of a summative, nationally accredited qualification that provides benchmarks of attainment.

Different types of assessment

◀ p. 118

The key to this was working in partnership with teachers and Music Services, drawing on their skills, experience and expertise. If the assessment can be undertaken by teachers themselves during normal lesson time, there are significant advantages all round, not least in increasing accessibility through reducing cost. In this way, the availability of Music Medals does not have to be dictated by the requirements of the academic year or the availability of an external examiner, and assessments can take place on any date and at any time of the teacher's choosing. After all, it is the teacher who best understands the pupil's individual strengths and weaknesses and who is best able to determine when formal assessment should take place.

Teams of instrumental consultants, who were both acknowledged experts in their field and experienced group teachers, worked to establish the technical and musical parameters for each Medal. Once an initial set of materials had been commissioned and moderated, a pilot scheme was run with over thirty Music Services throughout the UK. This provided invaluable feedback and an insight into the issues involved in the training of Teacher-Assessors. Of course this pilot also meant that the materials were extensively tried and tested by pupils, and their reactions informed the final selection of music and the associated tests and activities.

Structure

Ensemble

Making music together is a fundamental part of the Music Medals syllabus and is supported by the Associated Board's own dedicated Music Medals ensemble publications. These contain duets, trios and quartets in a very wide range of styles including well-known music, original compositions, pieces in jazz and pop idioms, traditional music, spirituals, and arrangements of Baroque and Classical music, as well as Romantic genre pieces. The content and titles of the pieces at the most elementary levels reflect the fact that they have been written with young learners in mind, but later on the 'child-friendly' element has been carefully considered; it decreases as the levels progress to avoid alienating older children or adult learners.

Music Medals allow ensemble skills to be introduced in a progressive way, recognizing that duets with the teacher will be the access point for many at Copper and Bronze levels. At the earliest stages of learning pupils will find holding a part in an ensemble a considerable challenge, so it is vital that they experience duet playing in a positive environment if they are to embrace the next step in ensemble playing with enthusiasm. For this reason, at these first two levels, teachers may contribute to any ensemble; thereafter, they may take a line in any trio or quartet. The 'one player per line' rule applies to the assessment of all Music Medals ensemble pieces. Of course, in the learning process teachers may want to treat the material more flexibly.

Instrumental technique and musical ability can often be greater than personal self-confidence in the early stages, so plenty of encouragement and support from the teacher is frequently necessary. But the goal here is to allow pupils increasing autonomy as their confidence grows. Music Medals encourage pupils to develop simple 'counting in' and 'bringing in' skills from as early on as possible, rather than the teacher acting as the group's director or conductor. If pupils are given the autonomy to lead the group and to take responsibility for its performance, they learn essential aspects of what it is to be a musician. This is reflected in two of the assessment criteria: 'interaction' (leading, eye contact, gesture and body language) and 'responsiveness to the group' (balance and blend, give and take, and negotiation). The positioning of players in relation to each other is, of course, crucial in facilitating the eye contact and communication that are vital parts of ensemble performance. Pupils who have learnt to play together in their instrumental lessons will have no difficulty in joining the larger ensembles run by their Music Service or school, or in the community.

6

Encouraging progress

Candidates are not obliged to use the Board's ensemble books for their Music Medals, as there is an additional list of items taken from tutor and method books selected for the Solo lists (see below). However, the Music Medals books present the music in full score, whereas many ensemble pieces in tutor books are presented as a series of parts. Playing from a full score is particularly useful in the group-teaching context as it:

- helps pupils understand their part in relation to the whole ensemble;
- enables discussion of compositional content and ensemble nuances;
- helps pupils to react more quickly to the mistakes of others;
- gives pupils the opportunity to learn all parts.

The Music Medals ensemble books accommodate mixed-ability groups and provide a set of pieces that pupils can use on an ongoing basis, rather than just for the purposes of gaining their Medal. Teachers of mixed-instrument groups may, at their discretion, arrange lines – other than that taken by the candidate – for alternative instruments, taking into account balance, timbre and related ensemble considerations. (Teachers wishing to do this must refer to the Regulations in the Music Medals Syllabus Handbook.) The technical level of individual lines within the ensemble material tends to be at a slightly lower level than that expected for the solo performance, as playing within an ensemble increases the difficulty of any individual line.

Solo

Performing as a soloist develops musical independence and individuality, and allows pupils to focus on their own sound as well as their personal expression. For the Medal assessment, the candidate may play either with an accompaniment (live or CD backing track) or unaccompanied. Pieces are chosen from the Board's extensive prescribed list, containing items selected from all commonly used tutor and method books. This list is updated as new teaching material is published and is available on the Music Medals website (http://www.musicmedals.org).

No value judgements have been made with regard to the relative merits of different pedagogical approaches, so the extensive repertoire lists are fully accessible to all group teachers. Within any level there is a certain range of technical and musical challenge that is acceptable and pieces have been selected if they fall within that range.

Pupils tend to be less nervous playing a solo in front of their friends than they are when performing to an external examiner. The presence of the video camera gives a sense of occasion, and for the Medal pupils may play to an audience wider than just members of the group if they wish. There is also the opportunity for pupils to announce their items. This builds confidence and provides a useful preparation for other performance occasions, such as playing for school assembly or to family and friends.

Options

In the final section of the Medal assessment, pupils are able to play to their strengths by choosing one of four Options: Call & Response, Make a Tune, Question & Answer or Sight-Reading. These have been arranged to cover the spectrum between a totally aural musical interaction and one that is based entirely on notation – what may be regarded as right-brain through to left-brain activity. They are designed to encourage all-round musicianship and to support the kinds of creative music-making that form part of all good group teaching. While it is in the nature of tests to impose restrictions, it is hoped that teachers will take flexible approaches to developing improvisation and not rigidly 'teach to the test'. The ways of working that are described in Chapter 8 are of particular relevance here.

The Options cover assessment of many skills, including: echoing a rhythm, 'thinking in sound', keeping a steady pulse while creating a tune, using pattern and shape, reading notation, and creative ability. They are all based on the pupil's developing knowledge and understanding of scales and his or her ability to recognize and respond to musical pattern and shape.

In conclusion

Music Medals form a set of accessible and cost-effective goals that measure progress and support the widening of musical opportunities for children. If they provide the motivation that enables pupils to travel faster and further during the early stages of their musical journey, then they are indeed a valuable resource. If they also raise the status of instrumental music within schools through making the celebration of pupils' achievements more visible, then benefits accrue to everyone involved in instrumental teaching and learning.

For full details of the requirements and regulations of Music Medals, please visit the Music Medals website (http://www.musicmedals.org).

Bibliography

Borland, John, *Musical Foundations. A Record of Musical Work in Schools and Training Colleges* (London: Oxford University Press, 1927).

Duckett, Richard, and Price, Gary, *Explorations: A Workbook of Musical Starting Points for Specialist Instrumental Teaching and Learning* (Bromsgrove, Worcs.: Team World Music Ltd, 2003).

Federation of Music Services/National Association of Music Educators, *A Common Approach 2002* (London: Faber Music, 2002).

Glover, Joanna, *Children Composing, 4–14* (London: Routledge, 2000).

Hallam, Susan, *Instrumental Teaching: A Practical Guide to Better Teaching and Learning* (Oxford: Heinemann, 1998).

Harris, Paul and Crozier, Richard, *The Music Teacher's Companion* (London: The Associated Board of the Royal Schools of Music, 2000).

Kyriacou, Chris, *Effective Teaching in Schools*, 2nd edn (Cheltenham: Stanley Thornes, 1997).

Lasserson, Nadia, *The Piano Needn't be Lonely* (privately published; available from 34 Carver Road, London SE24 9LT, tel. 020 7274 6821).

Mackworth-Young, Lucinda, *Tuning In: Practical Psychology for Musicians who are Teaching, Learning and Performing* (Houghton-on-the-Hill, Norfolk: Music, Mind and Movement, 2001).

Odam, George, *The Sounding Symbol: Music Education in Action* (Cheltenham: Stanley Thornes, 1995).

Qualifications and Curriculum Authority, *National Curriculum 2000* (London, 2000).

Subotnick, Morton, *Making Music*, CD-ROM (New York: Learn Technologies Interactive, *c*.1995).

Swanwick, Keith, *Teaching Music Musically* (London: Routledge, 1999).

The following websites contain useful information and guidance on issues discussed in this book.

British Educational Communications and Technology Agency (Becta): http://www.becta.org.uk

Department for Education and Skills (DfES): http://www.dfes.gov.uk

National Curriculum: http://www.nc.uk.net

National Grid for Learning (NGfL): http://www.ngfl.gov.uk (UK); http://www.ltscotland.org.uk/ngflscotland (Scotland); http://www.ngfl-cymru.org.uk (Wales)

Qualifications and Curriculum Authority: http://www.qca.org.uk (UK); http://www.accac.org.uk (Wales)

Virtual Teacher Centre: http://vtc.ngfl.gov.uk (UK); http://www.svtc.org.uk (Scotland); http://www.ngfl-cymru.org.uk/vtc-home (Wales)

Index

Page numbers in bold type indicate main references.